Understanding Potential Changes to the Veterans Equitable Resource Allocation (VERA) System

A Regression-Based Approach

Jeffrey Wasserman
Jeanne Ringel
Karen Ricci
Jesse Malkin
Barbara Wynn
Jack Zwanziger
Sydne Newberry
Marika Suttorp
Afshin Rastegar

Prepared for the Department of Veterans Affairs

NATIONAL DEFENSE RESEARCH INSTITUTE
and RAND HEALTH

The research described in this report was sponsored by the Department of Veterans Affairs (DVA). The research was conducted jointly by RAND Health's Center for Military Health Policy Research and the Forces and Resources Policy Center of RAND's National Defense Research Institute, a federally funded research and development center supported by the Office of the Secretary of Defense, the Joint Staff, the unified commands, and the defense agencies under Contract DASW01-01-C-0004.

Library of Congress Cataloging-in-Publication Data

Understanding potential changes to the Veterans Equitable Resource Allocation System (VERA) : a regression-based approach / Jeffrey Wasserman ... [et al.].
    p. cm.
    "MG-163."
    Includes bibliographical references.
    ISBN 0-8330-3560-6 (pbk. : alk. paper)
    1. Veterans—Medical care—United States. 2. Veterans Equitable Resource Allocation System. I. Wasserman, Jeffrey.

UB369.U5 2004
362.1'086'970973—dc22

2004001845

The RAND Corporation is a nonprofit research organization providing objective analysis and effective solutions that address the challenges facing the public and private sectors around the world. RAND's publications do not necessarily reflect the opinions of its research clients and sponsors.

RAND® is a registered trademark.

Published 2004 by the RAND Corporation
1700 Main Street, P.O. Box 2138, Santa Monica, CA 90407-2138
1200 South Hayes Street, Arlington, VA 22202-5050
201 North Craig Street, Suite 202, Pittsburgh, PA 15213-1516
RAND URL: http://www.rand.org/
To order RAND documents or to obtain additional information, contact
Distribution Services: Telephone: (310) 451-7002;
Fax: (310) 451-6915; Email: order@rand.org

Preface

In January of 2001, at the request of Congress, the Veterans Health Administration (VHA) asked RAND National Defense Research Institute (NDRI), a division of the RAND Corporation, to undertake a study of the Veterans Equitable Resource Allocation (VERA) system. Instituted in 1997, VERA was designed to improve the allocation of the congressionally appropriated medical care budget to the regional service networks that constituted the Department of Veterans Affairs (VA) health system. Phase I of this study was completed in nine months and provided a qualitative analysis of VERA. Findings and recommendations from Phase I are reported in *An Analysis of the Veterans Equitable Resource Allocation (VERA) System,* published by RAND (Wasserman et al.) in September 2001. In Phase I, an analysis plan was developed to conduct a quantitative analysis of VERA and the potential impact of modifications to VERA on the VA health system. At the request of Congress, the VHA asked NDRI to conduct the proposed quantitative analysis as Phase II of the project. The findings of the analysis were reported in *An Analysis of Potential Adjustments to the Veterans Equitable Resource Allocation (VERA) System*, published by RAND (Wasserman et al.) in January 2003. Again at the request of Congress, the VHA asked NDRI to conduct additional quantitative analyses to explore further the effects of patient and facility characteristics on costs of care and allocations. Study findings should be of interest to VA personnel, Congress, and other policymakers, particularly those interested in health care for veterans. Health economists and policy planners may also have an interest in the findings.

This research was sponsored by the Department of Veterans Affairs and was carried out jointly by RAND Health's Center for Military Health Policy Research and the Forces and Resources Policy Center of the NDRI. The latter is a federally funded research and development center sponsored by the Office of the Secretary of Defense, the Joint Staff, the unified commands, and the defense agencies.

Comments on this report should be directed to Jeffrey Wasserman, PhD, the principal investigator (Jeffrey@rand.org); Jeanne Ringel, coprincipal investigator (ringel@rand.org); or Karen Ricci, RN, MPH, the project director (karenri@rand.org). Susan Everingham, MA, is the director for RAND's Forces and Resources Policy Center (susane@rand.org), and C. Ross Anthony, PhD, is director of the RAND Center for Military Health Policy Research (rossa@rand.org).

The RAND Corporation Quality Assurance Process

Peer review is an integral part of all RAND research projects. Prior to publication, this document, as with all documents in the RAND monograph series, was subject to a quality assurance process to ensure that the research meets several standards, including the following: The problem is well formulated; the research approach is well designed and well executed; the data and assumptions are sound; the findings are useful and advance knowledge; the implications and recommendations follow logically from the findings and are explained thoroughly; the documentation is accurate, understandable, cogent, and temperate in tone; the research demonstrates understanding of related previous studies; and the research is relevant, objective, independent, and balanced. Peer review is conducted by research professionals who were not members of the project team.

RAND routinely reviews and refines its quality assurance process and also conducts periodic external and internal reviews of the quality of its body of work. For additional details regarding the RAND quality assurance process, visit http://www.rand.org/standards/.

Contents

Figure

Tables

Summary

Background and Approach

The Veterans Equitable Resource Allocation (VERA) system was instituted by the Veterans Health Administration (VHA) in 1997 in a continuing effort to improve the allocation of congressionally appropriated health care funds to the 21 Veterans Integrated Service Networks (VISNs).[1] VERA was designed to ensure that funds are allocated in an equitable, comprehensible, and efficient manner and to address the complexities of providing health care to veterans with service-connected disabilities, low incomes, and special health care needs.

In contrast to earlier VHA allocation systems, which were based largely on historical costs, VERA bases its allocation of funds primarily on the number of veterans served (workload). However, the veteran population has been shifting dramatically from some geographic areas to others. As a result, since the implementation of VERA, allocations to the VISNs have undergone similar shifts, from areas with shrinking veteran populations to areas with increasing numbers of veterans. These funding shifts prompted concerns in Congress that VERA was not distributing resources equitably across the VISNs, which could affect health care delivery to some veterans. In legislation enacted in late 2000 (Public Law No. 106-377), Congress directed the Department of Veterans Affairs (VA) to determine "whether VERA may lead to a distribution of funds that does not cover the special needs of some veterans." The VHA contracted with the RAND National Defense Research Institute to examine three specific areas of concern expressed by Congress:

- The extent to which allocations cover costs associated with maintaining older-than-average medical facilities, caring for populations with complex case mixes, facilities undergoing major consolidation, and/or rural versus urban location.
- Issues associated with maintaining affiliations between the VA medical centers and academic medical centers.
- The extent to which weather differences influence costs.

To address these issues within the allotted time, the NDRI initially conducted a qualitative analysis of the VERA system. Based on our review of the literature and interviews, we concluded that VERA appeared to meet its objectives of improving the allocation of resources to meet the geographical distribution of veterans as well as improving the incentive

---

[1] These VISNs span the United States, its territories, and the Philippines. In fiscal year (FY) 2002, the number of VISNs was reduced from 22 to 21 (VISNs 13 and 14 were combined to become VISN 23).

structure, fairness, and simplicity of the allocation methodology. We also found that the influence of several factors of concern to Congress on the costs of providing health care to veterans—the number of buildings, services offered, rural (versus urban) location, and extremes of weather—was unclear, or, in the case of weather extremes, not important. In contrast, we identified several factors that appeared to exert a predictable and systematic influence on veterans' health care costs. These factors included patient case mix and the presence or absence of facility affiliations with medical schools (findings from that analysis appear in the report *An Analysis of the Veterans Equitable Resource Allocation (VERA) System* [Wasserman et al., 2001]). However, the Phase I report also concluded that comprehensive evaluation of the current system, and of possible modifications to it, required extensive quantitative analysis.

At the request of Congress, we undertook a quantitative analysis of the VERA system (Phase II) to assess how a variety of patient, facility, and community characteristics affected costs of patient care; to create a model to assess the impact of a wide range of policy changes; and to simulate how such policy changes would affect VISN allocations. Our approach was to create multivariate regression models that included factors that might lead to differences in patient costs. One such model, the "all variables model" (AVM), included all variables we could identify that might influence differences in patient costs. Another model, the "selected variables model" (SVM), included only variables that showed a significant effect in our first model, that were consistent with the VA mission, and that were largely outside the control of VISN directors. Factors that were found to have a major influence on costs included patient case-mix measures, patient reliance on Medicare for coverage of health care, and a small number of facility variables. Based on these findings, we recommended that the VA consider modifying VERA to take greater account of patient and facility characteristics than it did. One mechanism for doing so would be to adopt an allocation system that relies on a regression/simulation framework similar to the one used in the Phase II analysis. However, before implementing such an allocation system, we recommended conducting additional analyses to gain a better understanding of how particular variables influence VISN allocations.

After examining the results of this second phase of research, Congress and the VHA requested that NDRI conduct a set of additional analyses. The goals of Phase III were to determine how particular patient and facility characteristics influence allocations to VISNs and to simplify and refine the models created in Phase II to reflect policy changes and more recent data. One such policy change was the fiscal year (FY) 2003 modification of VERA's case-mix adjustment mechanism from three categories (VERA-3) to ten categories (VERA-10).

Our approach was similar to that of Phase II, with several important differences:

- We used more recent data sets to estimate costs and to simulate VISN allocations.
- We simplified our modeling approach substantially by collapsing the patient- and facility-level equations into a single-equation model without sacrificing the power of our original two-equation model to explain and predict costs.
- To generate additional insights into our simulated VISN allocations, we disaggregated the results to show the influence of each variable included in the models on VISN allocations.

Using our regression equation, we constructed three types of models, with three distinct objectives.

Our first model, the "base regression model" (BRM), was intended to demonstrate how a regression-based approach for calculating VISN allocations compares with the method that the VA currently uses to arrive at the allocations. The BRM included only those variables that reflect the current types of adjustments that the VA takes into account in determining VISN allocations: a ten-group case-mix-adjustment measure, an index that measures geographic variation in the costs of labor inputs used to provide patient care, and measures for teaching intensity and research costs.

The second model, the all variables model (mentioned above), was designed to account for all patient, facility, and community variables that had been shown to influence the costs of treating veterans at VA health care facilities and that could be measured using readily available data sets.

Our third type of model, the selected variables model (mentioned above), included all of the variables found in the BRM, as well as some additional measures of patient and facility characteristics that were included in the AVM—that is, variables that were found to influence the costs of care and that might be appropriate to use for policy purposes. Only the findings for the SVM are summarized here.

In addition, to further assess the effects of case-mix measure, we compared the effects of the models using the VERA-10 case-mix measure with those using a more refined case-mix adjustment—VA diagnostic cost groups (DCGs).[2]

Findings

Regression Results

Six patient-level variables played key roles in explaining an individual's use of VA resources:

- Similar to the findings of the Phase II report, gender and age independently affected patient care costs when we controlled for case-mix and other factors. However, patients who were older than 85 had lower costs.
- Health status played a significant role in determining health costs.
- When VERA-10 was used as the adjustment for health status, patients residing in areas with greater concentrations of physicians and hospital beds incurred significantly higher health costs than those residing in areas with lower concentrations of health care providers.
- Patients who traveled a greater distance to receive their health care have higher costs.
- Greater Medicare reliance was associated with lower VA health costs.

A small number of facility-level characteristics also influenced individuals' use of VA health care resources:

---

[2] The VA DCGs are a modification of the standard DCGs that reflect differences between the veteran population and the privately insured population, for which off-the-shelf DCGs software is intended. Specifically, the VA combined 30 highest-ranked condition categories (HCCs) (those that are very uncommon in the VA population or do not predict significant positive costs) into one category and added 14 VERA category flags for special disability programs (e.g., spinal cord injury, traumatic brain injury, and serious mental illness). The VA then predicted the costs for each patient from the HCC model and assigned patients to one of 24 "VA DCGs" categories based on their predicted costs (VHA, 2001). In our equations that use DCGs, one dichotomous variable was included for each VA DCG except the lowest-cost VA DCG, which served as the reference group.

- VISN labor index, research costs per patient, and square feet of building space per patient had positive influences on costs; that is, they increased costs independently of the case-mix measure used.
- In contrast, for two variables in the SVM—number of residents per full-time physician and square feet of building space per acre of land—the direction of the association with costs depended on which health status measure was included in the model. When the VERA-10 measure was used, the number of residents per full-time physician had a positive effect on patient costs, but when the VA DCGs was used as the case-mix measure, it had a negative effect. Similarly, the square feet of building space per acre of land was positively associated with costs when VA-DCGs was the case-mix measure, but it was insignificant under VERA-10.

Simulation Results

The results from the BRM and SVM regression models were used to simulate VISN allocations. To interpret the simulation results, we made three types of comparisons. First, we compared actual FY 2003 allocations to the simulated allocations from the BRM, to isolate the effect of the difference between the actual VERA methodology and the regression-based methodology. Second, we compared the VERA-10 SVM allocations with the BRM allocations. Finally, we compared the VERA-10 SVM allocations with the VA DCG SVM allocations.

We found that recent VERA policy changes—including the introduction of the VERA-10 case-mix adjustment and the manner in which high-cost cases (i.e., those with costs of $70,000 or more) are treated under VERA—have reduced differences in the ways funds are allocated under the current VERA system compared with the regression-based approach. For example, in FY 2002, applying the regression-based approach—in particular, the VERA-10 SVM—would have redistributed 2.9 percent of the total actual allocation. However, in FY 2003, the regression-based approach with VERA-10 would have redistributed only 1.2 percent of the funds. VA DCGs would lead to a slightly larger redistribution (i.e., 1.8 percent of the total allocation).

Disaggregation Results

The disaggregation analysis compared the simulated allocation when each patient was assigned the average value for each characteristic (the "unadjusted average allocation") with the simulated allocation that occurs when a characteristic of interest (e.g., health status) was allowed to take its true value. The results can be viewed in two ways: from the VISN perspective and from the national perspective.

Viewing the results from the VISN perspective shows how each variable helps to move a particular VISN from the unadjusted average, or workload-based, allocation to the simulated allocations from the SVM.

Viewing the results from the national perspective shows the factors that are most important in affecting allocations nationwide. In general, there was a great deal of correspondence across case-mix specifications in terms of which variables appeared to move the most money around. In fact, the five variables that moved the most money around were the same, regardless of which case-mix measure was included in the model, although the order differed slightly between measures: health status, research costs per unique patient, the VA labor index, Medicare reliance, and the square feet of building space per patient. In both case-mix specifications, the amount of money redistributed by the health status measure far exceeded the amount redistributed by any other variable. The current VA system already adjusts for the top three money movers: health status, research costs, and geographic differences in labor costs.

Conclusions and Policy Implications

In general, the findings of this Phase III analysis were similar to those of Phase II.

A key conclusion from both the results presented in this report and those of the Phase II analysis is that case mix is critical in explaining differences in patients' costs and that it varies across VISNs. In Wasserman et al., 2003, we recommended that the VA adopt a more refined case-mix-adjustment methodology—either VERA-10 or VA DCGs—than the one it had used since VERA's inception, which relied on only three categories. Subsequently, the VA adopted the VERA-10 case-mix measure. We applaud this decision, as we believe that it will lead to a more efficient and equitable division of health care resources.

What is less clear, however, is whether VERA could be further improved by moving from VERA-10 to VA DCGs. On the one hand, VA DCGs better explain patient-level cost variation than does VERA-10. On the other hand, we observed that the VA DCGs would shift a substantial amount of money across VISNs, and we know little about why such redistributions would occur.

As we found in the Phase II analysis, Medicare reliance continues to have a statistically significant effect on the costs of treating veterans at VA facilities. Specifically, as one might expect, the greater the degree to which individuals rely on Medicare, the lower their VA costs. Consequently, we believe that the VA should consider modifying VISN allocations to adjust for differences in the degree to which VA patients rely on Medicare providers for the care they receive. Doing so would help make the VERA system more equitable and efficient. However, prior to implementing a Medicare reliance adjustment, we believe that the VA should investigate the accuracy with which Medicare data, which necessarily lag the VA data by a year, predict future Medicare expenditures.

Finally, in both this and the Phase II report, we used regression analysis to understand the extent to which a wide range of variables influences the costs of caring for VA patients. We believe that regression analysis holds great potential for serving as a mechanism for the VA to determine VISN-level allocations. However, we do not believe that it is critical at this juncture to shift to a regression-based allocation approach. The primary reason we advocate against such a transition at this point is that such a change would be difficult to implement, and the current allocation approach comes very close to the regression-based one, as evidenced by the low percentage of funds that the latter would redistribute. In the event that the VA elects to adjust VISN allocations for a wider range of variables—including, for example, Medicare reliance and some of the other factors that the disaggregation analysis demonstrated were responsible for shifting funds across VISNs—then adopting a regression-based approach might prove to be advantageous.

Even if the VA does not switch to a regression-based methodology, the use of regression analysis can provide a powerful management tool for VA headquarters staff and VISN directors. The single-equation approach upon which this study relied is easy to use and interpret. The output from the regression models can be used to identify additional potential adjustments to VERA, inform decisions regarding requests for supplemental funds, and provide guidance for VISN directors in determining how funds should be allocated to facilities within their networks.

Acknowledgments

We wish to express our deepest appreciation for the invaluable support we received throughout this project from our project officers at the Veterans Health Administration (VHA), John Vecciarelli and Paul Kearns. Without the extraordinary efforts they exerted to ensure timely access to the data, we could not have completed the project. In addition, they served as true partners, providing insightful feedback throughout the course of the project. We would also like to express our appreciation to Stephen Kendall and Robert McNamara of the VHA's Allocation Resource Center for fulfilling our data requests and adding analytical insights along the way. Thanks are also extended to John Vitikacs, Cortland Peret, and Susanne Mardres of VHA headquarters, who assisted us in a wide variety of ways during the course of the project; to Jim Burgess from the Management Sciences Group; and to Stephen Meskin, Chief Actuary of the VA. We are also indebted to the members of the VHA Steering Committee that was assembled to provide overall project guidance. We would like to thank Leigh Rohr for her assistance in preparing this manuscript and for providing general administrative support to the project. Finally, we have benefited greatly from the insightful comments we received from Peter D. Jacobson, Geoffrey Joyce, and Judith R. Lave on an earlier version of this report.

Acronyms and Abbreviations

ARC	Allocation Resource Center
ARF	Area Resource File
AVM	All Variables Model
BRM	Base Regression Model
Btu	British thermal unit
CBOC	Community-Based Outpatient Clinic
CPI	Consumer Price Index
DCGs	Diagnostic Cost Groups
DSS	Decision Support System
FFS	Fee for Service
FTE	Full-Time Equivalent Employee
FY	Fiscal Year
GI	Gastrointestinal
GP	General Purpose
HCC	Highest-Ranked Condition Category
HCFA	Health Care Financing Administration
HMO	Health Maintenance Organization
LTC	Long-Term Care
MSIS	Medical Statistical Information System
MSPE	Mean Squared Prediction Error
NDRI	National Defense Research Institute
NRM	Non-Recurring Maintenance
OLS	Ordinary Least Squares
PTSD	Posttraumatic Stress Disorder
SCI	Spinal Cord Injury
SVM	Selected Variables Model
VA	Department of Veterans Affairs
VERA	Veterans Equitable Resource Allocation
VHA	Veterans Health Administration
VISN	Veterans Integrated Service Network

CHAPTER ONE

Introduction

The Veterans Equitable Resource Allocation (VERA) system was instituted by the Veterans Health Administration (VHA) in 1997 in a continuing effort to improve the allocation of congressionally appropriated health care funds to the Veterans Integrated Service Networks (VISNs).[1] VERA was designed to ensure that funds are allocated in an equitable, comprehensible, and efficient manner and to address the complexities of providing health care to veterans with service-connected disabilities, low incomes, and special health care needs.

In contrast to earlier VHA allocation systems, which were based largely on historical costs, VERA bases its allocation of funds primarily on the number of veterans served (workload). However, the veteran population has been shifting dramatically from some geographic areas to others. As a result, since the implementation of VERA, allocations to the VISNs have undergone similar shifts, from areas with shrinking veteran populations to areas with increasing numbers of veterans. These funding shifts prompted concerns in Congress that VERA was not distributing resources equitably across the VISNs, which could affect health care delivery to some veterans. In legislation enacted in late 2000 (Public Law No. 106-377), Congress directed the Department of Veterans Affairs (VA) to determine "whether VERA may lead to a distribution of funds that does not cover the special needs of some veterans." The VHA contracted with the RAND National Defense Research Institute (NDRI), a division of the RAND Corporation, to examine three specific areas of concern expressed by Congress:

- The extent to which allocations cover costs associated with maintaining older-than-average medical facilities, caring for populations with complex case mixes, facilities undergoing major consolidation, and/or rural versus urban location.
- Issues associated with maintaining affiliations between the VA medical centers and academic medical centers.
- The extent to which weather differences influence costs.

To address these issues, the NDRI initially conducted a qualitative analysis of the VERA system. Findings from that analysis, which appear in the report *An Analysis of the Veterans Equitable Resource Allocation (VERA) System* (Wasserman et al., 2001), are summarized below (see Findings of Phase I and II Reports). A primary finding of the Phase I report was that comprehensive evaluation of the current system, and of possible modifications to it, required extensive quantitative analysis. At the request of Congress, NDRI undertook a quanti-

---

[1] These VISNs span the United States, its territories, and the Philippines. In fiscal year (FY) 2002, the number of VISNs was reduced from 22 to 21.

tative analysis of the VERA system (Phase II) to assess how patient, facility, and community characteristics affected costs of patient care; to create a model to assess the impact of a wide range of policy changes; and to simulate how such policy changes would affect VISN allocations. After examining the results of this second phase of research, which are summarized below (see Findings of Phase I and II Reports), Congress and the VHA requested that NDRI conduct a set of additional analyses to determine how particular patient and facility characteristics influence allocations to VISNs and to simplify and refine the models created in Phase II to reflect policy changes and more recent data.

Description of the VERA System[2]

VERA represents VHA's most recent effort to implement a resource allocation system that is both equitable and efficient and that preserves, if not enhances, VHA's commitment to providing high-quality health care to the veteran population. VERA allocates most of the congressional appropriation to VHA for health care—over $23 billion in fiscal year (FY) 2003—to the 21 regional networks nationwide (see the figure). To do so, it first divides the appropriation into General Purpose funding and Specific Purpose funding.

General Purpose funds are allocated according to a number of factors: the number and type of patients treated, geographic price adjustments, research support, education support, equipment, and non-recurring maintenance (NRM), as well as two new factors added in FY 2003: adjustments for the highest-cost patients and establishment of minimum/maximum caps on allocation increases. In FY 2003, these funds accounted for approximately 86 percent ($20.5 billion) of the congressional appropriation. Specific Purpose funds ($3.4 billion in FY 2003) finance the costs associated with programs that are administered by VHA headquarters. These programs include, for example, the provision of prosthetic devices, quality improvement initiatives, and database development, as well as the headquarters' centralized programs expenses. A portion of the Specific Purpose funds is held in reserve to cover contingencies that may arise during the course of the fiscal year.

Determination of Patient Care Allocations

Three factors related to patient care are considered for allocation purposes: patient groups (case mix), workload (the volume of patients treated in each patient group), and price setting (the dollar value determined by the volume and patient group).

Patient Groups. For purposes of calculating a VISN's patient care allocation, patients are classified into two main categories, Basic Care and Complex Care. In FY 2003, the case-mix adjustment was refined by further subdividing these two categories into 10 price groups;[3] the new case-mix adjustment methodology is referred to as VERA-10. (Appendix A contains a description of the formulas used to allocate VERA funds in FY 2003.)

---

[2] See *An Analysis of the Veterans Equitable Resource Allocation (VERA) System* (Wasserman et al., 2001) for a more complete description of VERA.

[3] From 1997 to 1998, patients were divided into only two cost groups: Basic Care and Complex Care. A third price group, Basic Single Outpatient Visit, was established for 1999 only. Beginning in 2000 and until 2003, Basic Care patients were divided into two groups, Basic Vested and Basic Non-Vested, resulting in a total of three cost groups. The Basic Vested category included patients with routine health care needs who either were hospitalized in a VA facility or received a comprehensive physical examination from a VA provider during the prior three years. The Basic Non-Vested category included

Veterans Health Administration Map of VISN Locations

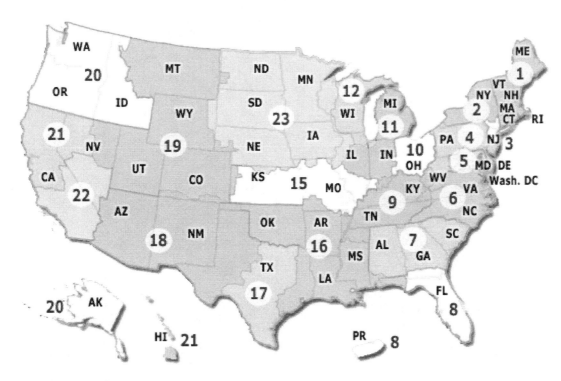

SOURCE: VHA web site.

NOTE: During FY 2002, two VISNs, 13 and 14, were consolidated to form VISN 23.

RAND*MG163-1.1*

Basic Care patients are "those who have relatively 'routine' health care needs. They are principally cared for in the ambulatory care setting, with short-term inpatient admissions, as necessary. They generally do not require the services of special emphasis programs" (VERA Book, 2003, p. 4). Basic Care patients' health care needs range from the simple to the complex, and include both acute and chronic conditions. Basic Care patients are further divided into six price groups (Table 1.1): Non-Reliant Care (encompassing the former Basic Non-Vested patients as well as some Basic Vested patients with minimal health care needs); Basic Medical; Mental Health; Heart, Lung, and Gastrointestinal (GI); Oncology; and Multiple Problem. Some 96 percent of VA patients are in the Basic Care categories and account for 67 percent of patient care dollars (VERA Book, 2003, p. 4).

The Complex Care category includes the other 4 percent of VA patients who require substantial (often inpatient) health care resources to treat a chronic illness or disabling condition, generally over a long time period. Many Complex Care patients were treated in one of the VHA's special emphasis programs, such as spinal cord injury or posttraumatic stress disorder. Complex Care patients are further divided into four price groups: Specialized Care, Supportive Care, Chronic Mental Illness, and Critically Ill (Table 1.1).

---

patients with relatively routine health care needs who used some VA health services but did not receive inpatient services and did not receive a comprehensive medical evaluation by the VA system in the previous three years. This patient classification system was referred to as VERA-3.

Table 1.1
Capitation Rates for VERA-10 Price Groups for FY 2003

VERA-10 Group Number and Name	Capitation Rate
Basic Care	
1. Non-Reliant Care: Non-Vested/Vested	$263
2. Basic Medical: Vested	$2,413
3. Mental Health: Vested	$3,562
4. Heart, Lung, and GI: Vested	$3,722
5. Oncology: Vested	$8,337
6. Multiple Problem: Vested	$7,935
Complex Care	
7. Specialized Care	$18,751
8. Supportive Care	$29,780
9. Chronic Mental Illness	$39,448
10. Critically Ill	$61,177

SOURCE: Adapted from the VERA Book, 2003.

Workload Determination. VERA workload for Basic Care patients is based on utilization over the prior three years. However, one group—Basic Care patients in Priority Groups 7 and 8 whose illness is not service connected—is not included (the priority groups define the order of priority for enrollment, with Group 1 conferring the highest priority).[4] For Complex Care patients, the workload forecast is based on the number of Complex Care patients using VA medical services during the preceding five years.

Price Setting. The VA establishes a national price for each of the ten patient groups by taking VERA's annual budget allocation for each group and dividing by the expected national workload in each group. For FY 2003, the budget allocation for each group is based on the ratio of actual FY 2001 costs for that group to total costs; the source of cost data is the VA's Decision Support System (DSS). The allocation to a particular VISN for care of patients in any category is the product of the VISN's workload estimate and the national price for that care category. Adjustments to this figure are then made for geographic variation in the costs of non-contracted and contracted labor and contracted goods and services such as energy-related products, utilities, and provisions.[5] Table 1.2 shows the total funding and the national prices for the ten cost groups for FY 2003.

Other Expenses Covered by General Purpose Funds

In addition to covering the costs associated with patient care, VERA allocated over $1.6 billion to the VISNs in FY 2003 to support research, education, equipment purchases, and NRM expenses. Research support allocations to the networks for FY 2003 totaled $400 million and were distributed to the networks based on their research activity and the national

---

[4] More precisely, Basic Care Priority 7 and 8 patients who are not counted as VERA workload include those veterans who have incomes and net worth at or above an established threshold, whose illness/injury is not service connected, and who do not fall within Priority Groups 1 through 6. They are expected to pay specified copayments for the care they receive. Throughout this report, we refer to these patients as Basic Care Priority 7s or Priority 7 veterans.

[5] Prior to 2002, a geographic adjustment was made only for non-contracted labor; geographic adjustments for contracted labor and non-labor contracted goods and services were instituted in FY 2002.

Table 1.2
Establishing VERA National Prices for FY 2003

Total Budget	Basic Care	Budget	Workload[a]	National Price[b]
	1. Non-Reliant	$116,547	443,477	$263
	2. Basic Medical	$4,169,216	1,727,650	$2,413
	3. Mental Health	$1,076,150	302,092	$3,562
	4. Heart, Lung, & GI	$2,910,016	781,904	$3,722
	5. Oncology	$889,650	106,711	$8,337
	6. Multiple Problem	$3,317,072	418,053	$7,935
61%	Total	$12,478,652	3,779,887[c]	Weighted average $3,301
	Complex Care	**Budget**	**Workload[a]**	**National Price[b]**
	7. Specialized Care	$926,779	49,425	$18,751
	8. Supportive Care	$1,703,614	57,207	$29,780
	9. Chronic Mental Illness	$1,037,311	26,296	$39,448
	10. Critically Ill	$1,395,489	22,811	$61,117
24%	Total	$5,063,194	155,739[c]	Weighted average $32,511
	High-Cost Adjustment for Top 1%			
7%	$1,395,135 (Basic Care $252,523 [18%], Complex Care $1,142,612 [82%])			
	Research, Education, and NRM		2% Research support ($400 million)	
8%	$1,588,547		2% Education support ($356 million)	
			2% Equipment ($578 million)	
			1% NRM ($255 million)	

SOURCE: Adapted from the VERA Book, 2003.
NOTES: Total VA health care budget = $23.9 billion. 86 percent of General Purpose funds = $20.5 billion. 14 percent of Specific Purpose funds = $3.4 billion.
[a] Number of patients.
[b] Budget divided by number of patients. The national prices reflect the fact that the national price for each VISN is subject to a geographic price adjustment based on the cost of labor in that area.
[c] Basic Care patients represent 96 percent of total patients; Complex Care patients represent 4 percent.

price for research support. Education support ($356 million for 2003) is allocated on the basis of the number of approved residents per VISN. In contrast, equipment and NRM funds are allocated strictly on the basis of workload, although NRM is adjusted for geographic differences in construction costs. The total allocations for equipment and NRM for 2003 are $578 million and $255 million, respectively.

Other FY 2003 Changes to the VERA Allocation Methodology

As mentioned above, the VA instituted two additional changes to the VERA allocation methodology for FY 2003.

Adjustment for the Top 1 Percent of High-Cost Patients. Beginning in FY 2003, VISNs receive additional allocations for patients whose yearly costs exceed $70,000. More specifically, for high-cost patients, the VISN is reimbursed the appropriate VERA-10 prices and 100 percent of all costs exceeding $70,000. For example, consider a Basic Care patient in the Multiple Problem category (VERA category number 6) whose annual costs total $75,000. The VISN will receive $7,935, the national price for an individual in the Multiple Problem category, and an additional $5,000 for the costs incurred over and above $70,000.

Maximum and Minimum Caps on Allocation Increases. This provision assures that all VISNs will receive at least 5 percent more in FY 2003 than they received in FY 2002. To subsidize the increases for VISNs whose allocations did not grow by at least 5 percent, funding increases for fast-growing VISNs have been capped at 12.6 percent over their FY 2002 allocation.

Findings of Phase I and II Reports

In Phase I, we conducted an extensive literature review followed by site visits to VISNs and facilities throughout the continental United States, where we interviewed some 175 stakeholders (staff and administrators). Based on our review of the literature and interviews, we concluded that VERA appeared to meet its objectives of improving allocation of resources for the geographic distribution of veterans as well as improving the incentive structure, fairness, and simplicity of the allocation methodology. We also found that the influence of several factors of concern to Congress on the costs of providing health care to veterans—the number of buildings, services offered, rural (versus urban) location, and extremes of weather—was unclear, or, in the case of weather extremes, not important. In contrast, we identified several factors that appeared to exert a predictable and systematic influence on veterans' health care costs. These factors included patient case mix and the presence or absence of affiliations with medical schools.

The goal of Phase II was to conduct a quantitative analysis aimed at evaluating the impact of a wide range of patient and facility characteristics on the variation in patient costs across VISNs and to assess the potential effects of modifications that might be made to VERA to account for such factors. Our approach was to create multivariate regression models that included factors that might lead to differences in patient costs. One such model, the "all variables model" (AVM), included all variables we could identify that might influence differences in patient costs. Another model, the "selected variables model" (SVM), included only variables that showed a significant effect in our first model, were consistent with the VA mission, and were largely outside the control of VISN directors.[6] Using patient data from the VA, as well as data on veterans' Medicare expenditures from the Centers for Medicare and Medicaid Services and data on county health care resources from the Area Resource File (ARF) (Health Resources and Services Administration, 2001), we ran the models to estimate the effects of various patient- and facility-level factors on patient care costs. The models were also designed so that the results could be used to simulate the effects of various policy changes on VISN-level allocations.

Factors that were found to have a major influence on costs included patient case-mix measures, Medicare reliance,[7] and a small number of facility variables. Based on these findings, we recommended that the VA should consider modifying VERA to take greater account of patient and facility characteristics than it did. One mechanism for doing so would be to adopt an allocation system that relies on a regression/simulation framework similar to the one used in the Phase II analysis. However, before implementing such an allocation system, we recommended conducting additional analyses to gain a better understanding of how particular variables influence VISN allocations.

---

[6] In the Phase II report, the AVM was called the "Fully Specified Model," and the SVM was called the "Policy Model."

[7] Medicare reliance is measured as the percentage of total health care costs (Medicare payments, including beneficiary cost-sharing amounts, plus VA costs) that is covered by Medicare.

Phase III Objectives

The aim of Phase III of this project was to conduct further analyses to determine how particular patient and facility characteristics influence allocations. The analyses performed for Phase III were similar in many respects to those conducted under Phase II; however the Phase III analyses differed in several important ways.

First, the Phase III analyses used more recent data sets to estimate costs and to simulate VISN allocations. The Phase III analyses also reflected the recent adoption of the VERA-10 case-adjustment mechanism.

Second, we simplified our modeling approach substantially, without sacrificing our power to explain and predict costs. In Phase II, we developed two equations. The first equation estimated the effects of a number of patient-level factors on patient costs. One of these factors, facility-specific cost shifts, then became the dependent variable in a second equation to determine the facility-level factors that influenced the contribution of the treatment facility to patient costs. In Phase III, we combined the patient-level and facility-level equations into one equation. We then used this equation to predict each veteran's annual costs and used the predictions to simulate VISN allocations.

Third, to generate additional insights into our simulated VISN allocations, we disaggregated the results of our simulation to show the dollar influence of each variable included in the models on VISN allocations. That is, we compared each VISN's simulated allocations with what that VISN would have received if each of its patients and facilities had the national average values for all of the variables included in the models.

The remainder of this report is organized into three chapters and three appendixes. Chapter Two describes our analytic approach and the sources of data used in the analyses. Chapter Three presents the results of the analyses. Chapter Four presents our conclusions and a discussion of policy implications. Appendix A contains the key formulas and data from the FY 2003 VERA. Appendix B presents the VISN-level patient variables and descriptive statistics for FY 2001. In Appendix C, we show the supplemental regression and simulation model results.

CHAPTER TWO

Data Sources and Methods

We used a variety of quantitative analytic techniques to measure the impact of patient and facility characteristics on the costs of providing care to veterans. Specifically, our analyses were designed to incorporate the factors specified in the legislation authorizing this study, factors that emerged from the qualitative analysis that formed the basis of Phase I of the study, and findings from the Phase II analysis.

Our analytic approach closely resembles the approach that we took in the Phase II analysis. The analysis was structured to yield clear, policy-relevant, practical conclusions for the VA and other policymakers. The analytical approaches we used accounted for a large set of patient- and facility-level characteristics that might influence patient care costs. Here, we believed it was important to identify whether particular variables had a statistically significant effect on the costs of care and how VISN allocations would change in response to our attempts to adjust, or control for, a wide range of variables.

Although the analyses conducted under Phase II and those reported here are similar in many ways, there are also some important differences. First, in the present analysis we used more recent data sets to estimate costs and to simulate VISN allocations. Second, as will be described below, we simplified our modeling approach substantially, without sacrificing our power to explain and predict costs. Third, to generate additional insights into our simulated VISN allocations, we disaggregated the results to show the dollar influence of each variable included in the models on VISN allocations.

Overview of Analytic Methods

This section describes the motivations for our analytic approach and summarizes our methods. Subsequent sections in this chapter describe our analyses, including data and statistical methods, in detail.

Regression Equations

We began the analysis by constructing a set of patient- and facility-level regression equations similar to those used in the Phase II analysis. The equations were used to examine factors that affect the costs of treating patients at VA health care facilities. Specifically, the regression analysis, described more completely below, was used to explain variation in veterans' annual costs of care—including inpatient, outpatient, and long-term care costs—as a function of sociodemographic variables, health status measures, the availability of alternative sources of care, and the facility (or facilities, in the case of some veterans) where care was delivered. Table 2.1 lists the patient-level variables.

In the second stage of the analysis, we focused on identifying treatment facility characteristics that affect patient costs. We used the estimates for the facility variables that we obtained from the patient-level regression equations as the dependent variable in a set of facility regression equations. That is, the facility-level analysis was aimed at explaining the extent to which various facility characteristics accounted for differences in veterans' costs *after controlling for differences in the characteristics of the veterans served by each facility.* Thus, the facility equations attempted to explain cost differences as a function of each facility's location, infrastructure characteristics, labor and non-labor prices, medical school affiliations, research programs, and consolidation activity. Table 2.1 lists the facility-level variables.

In the third stage of the analysis, we used the patient- and facility-level regression equations we derived in stages one and two to predict each veteran's total annual costs, after controlling for both patient and facility characteristics. We then aggregated predicted patient costs at the VISN level and simulated how VISN allocations would vary after controlling for the variables included in the regression equations.

Once we selected the patient and facility variables to be included in the analysis, we simplified the analysis by developing a single-equation approach that combined the same patient- and facility-level characteristics used in the two-equation approach into one regression equation. We then used this equation to predict each veteran's annual costs and used the predictions to simulate VISN allocations. The simulation process is based on the annual predicted costs for each VISN, which can be calculated using either the single- or two-equation approach.[1] As will be described in Chapter Three, this single-equation approach performed as well as the two-equation approach and is much easier to estimate and interpret. Therefore, the analysis described below relied exclusively on the single-equation method.

Using the regression equation, we constructed three types of models, with three distinct objectives in mind (see Table 2.2). Our first model, which we refer to as the "base regression model" (BRM), was intended to demonstrate how a regression-based approach for calculating VISN allocations compares with the method that the VA currently uses to arrive at the allocations. Toward this end, we included only a very limited set of variables in the model: those variables that reflect the current types of adjustments that the VA takes into account in determining VISN allocations. These variables include a ten-group case-mix measure (VERA-10), an index that measures geographic variation in the costs of labor inputs used to provide patient care, and measures for teaching intensity and research costs (VERA Book, 2003).

In a sense, the BRM represents our best effort to model the status quo, where only a small number of adjustments are made to what is essentially a set of national prices for ten case types. At the other extreme is a model that we refer to as the AVM. In constructing this model, we attempted to account for all patient, facility, and community variables that we believed—based on an extensive review of the relevant literature and the Phase I case studies—influence the costs of treating veterans at VA health care facilities and that could be measured using readily available data sets.[2]

---

[1] For a detailed description of the two-equation approach, see Chapter Two of Wasserman et al., 2003.

[2] A discussion of the literature is contained in Wasserman et al., 2003; and the case study analysis is presented in Wasserman et al., 2001.

Table 2.1
Patient and Facility Explanatory Variables Used in Regression Equations

Variable	Reasons for Exclusion from SVM
Patient-level variables	
Health status/case-mix measure	
Age	
Gender	
Physicians per capita	
Hospital beds per capita	
Rural or urban status	
Distance to closest facility	
Distance to closest CBOC	
Medicare reliance	
Medicare imputation indicator	
Medicaid generosity—long-term care	
Facility indicator	
VA priority	Adjusting payment for VA priority status would be inconsistent with current VA policies
Income	Potential measurement error
Race/ethnicity	Adjusting payment for race/ethnicity would be inconsistent with VA mission/values
Marital status	Potential measurement error; adjusting payment for marital status would be inconsistent with VA mission/values
Medicaid generosity—general	Potential measurement error
Facility-level variables	
Residents per full-time physician	
VA labor index	
Research costs per 1,000 unique patients	
Average food cost per bed day	
Energy price (dollars per million Btus)	
Contract labor costs	
Square feet of building space per acre of land	
Square feet of building space per unique patient	
Rural or urban status	
Percentage of funded research	Not statistically significant and largely controllable by local VA managers
Average building age as of 2001	Not statistically significant
Average building condition	Not statistically significant
Leased square feet per patient	Inconsistent with current VA policies
Ratio of historic to total number of buildings	Not statistically significant
Total number of buildings	Not statistically significant
Indicator for recent facility/management consolidation	Not statistically significant and controllable
Occupancy rate	Inconsistent with current VA policies and not statistically significant
Number of CBOCs per 1,000 unique patients	Inconsistent with current VA policies
Direct patient care FTEs per 1,000 unique patients	Largely controllable by local VA managers
Non-patient care FTEs per 1,000 unique patients	Largely controllable by local VA managers
Long-term care beds per 1,000 unique patients	Inconsistent with current VA policies
Special program beds per 1,000 unique patients	Not statistically significant

NOTES: CBOC is community-based outpatient clinic. Btu is British thermal unit. FTE is full-time equivalent employee.

Key
Base, selected, and all variables models
Selected and all variables models
All variables model only

Table 2.2
Descriptions of Models Used in Analysis

Model	Description
BRM	Regression equation–based methodology that represents effort to take into account factors included in the current VERA allocation methodology; includes only variables that measure patient health status, research, and education costs; adjusts for geographic variation in labor and non-labor costs
AVM	Regression equation model designed to provide the best possible explanation of variation in patient care costs; includes variables believed to influence the costs of care and for which data were reasonably available
SVM	Regression equation model intended to be more appropriate for policy purposes than the AVM. The SVM contains a subset of the patient and facility variables included in the AVM

Our third type of model, the SVM, included all of the variables found in the BRM, as well as some additional measures of patient and facility characteristics that were included in the AVM. Specifically, we included variables that were found to influence the costs of care and that might be appropriate to use for policy purposes. In constructing this model, we included variables contained in the AVM that (1) were statistically significant;[3] (2) were consistent with the VA's mission, vision, or values; (3) were measured without significant error; and/or (4) met current VA policy objectives. For example, variables related to efficiency considerations (e.g., the number of full-time equivalent employees [FTEs] per 1,000 patients) were not included in the SVM because they were deemed to be largely within the control of the VISN management. We reasoned that statistically controlling for such variables might lead to an undesirable set of financial incentives that reward inefficient behavior.

It is important to note that the AVM and the SVM can potentially serve several purposes. For example, the AVM could be used to generate insight into the VERA supplemental, or adjustment, process. That is, because the AVM attempts to explain as much of the variation in costs as possible, it could be applied to assess the degree to which a VISN's request for supplemental funding is due to factors within or beyond the director's control. In contrast, the SVM could be used to assess the implications of various policy changes on VISN allocations. For instance, the model could be used to assess how allocations would change if they were adjusted for elderly veterans' Medicare expenditures. In fact, because Medicare reliance among veterans is increasing as the veteran population ages, we have chosen to include a measure of Medicare use in our AVM and SVM. Because the SVM has greater utility from a policy standpoint, we have chosen to focus our discussion of the results of our analysis contained in Chapter Three on that model. The results of the AVM are found in Appendix C.

Case-Mix Measures

As discussed in the first chapter, one of the ways that VERA seeks to ensure that resources are allocated equitably is by adjusting for differences in the health status of patients within each VISN. VERA-10, the current case-mix-adjustment mechanism, assigns patients to one of ten categories according to their level of health care use, basing capitation rates for each

---

[3] The statistical significance criterion for variables to be included in the SVM was based on the results of the two-equation approach to avoid the problems associated with the clustering of individuals in facilities (e.g., underestimating the standard errors of the facility-level variables in the regression equation).

category on the expected costs of the care for patients in each of the ten categories. These ten categories and their corresponding capitation rates are shown in Table 1.1.

An ongoing goal of our study of the VERA system was to determine whether VERA adequately accounts for differences in case mix across the VISNs. In our earlier reports, we suggested that the VERA system could benefit from adopting either VERA-10 or a case-mix measurement system based on diagnostic cost groups (DCGs) in place of the case-mix measure that accompanied the introduction of VERA and which relied on only three categories. Beginning with fiscal year 2003, the VA adopted VERA-10. As a result, we have incorporated VERA-10 into our BRM, and we have also used it as one of two alternative case-mix measures in our AVM and SVM. The second alternative case-mix measure used in these models is one based on a VA-adapted version of DCGs,[4] which we refer to as VA DCGs.

Data Sources

Our analyses relied on patient-, facility-, and county-level data.

Patient-Level Data

The patient-level data set was prepared by VHA's Allocation Resource Center (ARC), using a set of specifications we supplied to the VA. The ARC data set contains information on the annual costs of treating each patient at each VA facility, along with a host of patient-level socioeconomic, eligibility, cost, and health status variables. The cost measure included in the data set was taken from the VA's 2001 DSS database and is based on individuals' VA health care use (see Yu and Barnett, 2000, for a detailed description of the DSS database).

The patient-level file also contains information on individual Medicare "reliance" and county-level health care resources. Patient-level data on annual Medicare expenditures for users of the VA health system (which we refer to as "Medicare reliance") were available to RAND through agreements with the Centers for Medicare & Medicaid Services and the VA's Management Science Group.

Individual-level data on Medicaid expenditures for patients in the VA health care system are not readily available.[5] As a substitute, we created state-level measures of Medicaid generosity using data on state-level Medicaid expenditures and the number of poor adults in each state. The data on Medicaid expenditures came from the Center for Medicare & Medicaid Services (collected as part of the Medicaid Statistical Information System). State-level data on the number of adults living below the poverty line were taken from the Kaiser Family Foundation web site (www.kff.org). These data were based on estimates from the U.S. Census Bureau's 2001 *Current Population Survey.*

---

[4] The VA DCGs are a modification of the standard DCGs that reflect differences between the veteran population and the privately insured population, for which off-the-shelf DCGs software is intended. Specifically, the VA combined 30 highest-ranked condition categories (HCCs) (those that are very uncommon in the VA population or do not predict significant positive costs) into one category and added 14 VERA category flags for special disability programs (e.g., spinal cord injury, traumatic brain injury, and serious mental illness). The VA then predicted the costs for each patient from the HCC model and assigned patients to one of 24 "VA DCGs" categories based on their predicted costs (VHA, 2001). In our equations that use DCGs, one dichotomous variable was included for each VA DCG except the lowest-cost VA DCG, which served as the reference group.

[5] Ideally, we would have liked to include a measure for private health care insurance as well. However, this data element was not included in any of the data sources used in the analysis and could not be obtained from other existing data files.

Information on the local (i.e., county-level) supply of physicians and hospital beds was obtained from the 2001 ARF (Health Resources and Services Administration, 2001). The ARF data are produced annually by Quality Resource Systems, Inc., under contract to the Health Resources and Services Administration.

Facility-Level Data

The majority of the data on facility characteristics came from either the ARC or VA headquarters. Again, these files were constructed based on a set of specifications that RAND submitted to the VA. The facility file contains data on each facility's structural characteristics, costs, and staffing levels. We supplemented these data with information on state-level energy prices from the *State Energy Price Report* (U.S. Department of Energy, 2000). Information on the rural or urban status of the parent VA facility's location was obtained from the ARF.

Because some veterans received care at more than one facility, we aggregated each veteran's costs across facilities to obtain one observation per person. The facility characteristics included in the regression equation represent a weighted average across all facilities at which the individual was treated.[6]

Dependent and Explanatory Variables

In this section, we describe the dependent and explanatory variables that we used in the regression equations. We used the same dependent variables—DSS cost per patient—in the BRM, AVM, and SVM. However, as indicated previously, each of the three models contained a different set of explanatory variables.

Dependent Variables

The main focus of our analysis was on explaining how patient and facility characteristics affect the costs of providing health care to veterans. Consequently, the dependent variable used in our equations was the VA's annual cost of providing health care to the individual.[7] The costs included all medical care costs (inpatient, outpatient, and long-term care), as well as education and research support costs, resident salaries, equipment costs, and NRM costs.

As of FY 2003, the VA modified the VERA allocation policy to augment its allocation to VISNs with the highest-cost patients, that is, patients with costs over $70,000. VISNs with such patients will receive an additional allocation equal to the amount by which the patients' costs exceed $70,000. To reflect this change, we truncated the cost data at $70,000 for the regression analysis. That is, for those individuals who had annual costs of $70,000 or more, we set their costs equal to $70,000. The high-cost patient adjustment is then made in the simulation process after the regression has been estimated and predicted costs have been calculated.

---

[6] For example, suppose a person was treated at two facilities during the year and that his total costs were split such that 70 percent of costs were incurred at Facility A and 30 percent at Facility B. In this case, the facility characteristics included in the regression equation would be calculated as a weighted average between Facilities A and B, where Facility A receives a weight of 0.70 and Facility B receives a weight of 0.30.

[7] The VA's ARC used data contained in its DSS to allocate costs to patients. A description of this methodology can be found in Wasserman et al., 2003.

We note one issue that may be important for interpretation. DSS estimates the costs of individual health care encounters using data on the use and cost of intermediate products (e.g., a chest X-ray, a day in a medical ward, or a minute in the operating room). DSS then "normalizes" the cost estimates to the VA's cost allocation system so that when aggregated, the dollar costs sum to the relevant VA budget allocation. However, the VA budget allocation is not necessarily identical to the economic costs of producing the medical care products and services that were used by VA patients within that unit. As a result, our dependent variable can be thought of most appropriately as being derived from relative value weights for the underlying health care used by VA patients, rather than as estimates of the absolute economic cost of production.

Explanatory Variables

Table 2.1 lists the explanatory variables used in the regression equations. The table also shows which variables are included in the BRM, AVM, and SVM. The BRM contains only four variables. In contrast, the AVM contains 39 variables, 17 of which are measured at the patient level and the remaining 22 at the facility level. Deleting variables that failed one or more of the criteria for inclusion in the SVM left a total of 21 variables—12 variables that measured patient characteristics and 9 that measured facility characteristics.

Description of Selected Variables in the Regression Equations

Many of the variables included in the regressions are straightforward and do not warrant discussion (e.g., age, race/ethnicity, gender). However, some of the variables require more-detailed descriptions.

The regression equations contain two measures of county-level health care resources: hospital beds and physicians per capita. These measures were taken from the ARF and were matched to individual veterans based on their home zip code. Similarly, the measures of distance (in miles) to the facility at which the individual was treated and to the closest community-based outpatient clinic (CBOC) were calculated using the home zip code of the individual and the zip code of the facility or CBOC.[8] We used these variables to explore whether the availability of other health care resources in the county in which the veteran resides and the distance the veteran must travel to receive VHA services affect the amount of care the veteran obtains from VHA facilities.

Medicare reliance was measured as the percentage of total health care costs (Medicare payments, including beneficiary cost-sharing amounts, plus VA costs) that is covered by Medicare.[9] A person is said to be more reliant on Medicare as this percentage increases. The regression equation for the AVM also includes two measures of state Medicaid generosity. To obtain measures of generosity that are relevant for the VA population, we first created a general measure that is based on state-level Medicaid expenditures on recipients who are eligible for coverage because they are elderly, blind, or disabled. To incorporate information about a state's breadth of coverage, we scaled the expenditures by the number of poor adults (age 18

---

[8] The distance is calculated from the center of the home zip code to the center of the facility's zip code. The precise methodology used to calculate these distances came from Meridian World Data and is described at www.meridianworlddata.com/HTML9/distance-calculate-2.asp.

[9] Controlling for Medicare reliance is potentially important because failure to do so may lead to inequitable allocations across VISNs, because people presenting with similar diagnoses will consume different levels of resources depending on the degree that they receive services from Medicare providers.

and over) in the state. The resulting measure (expenditures per poor adult) incorporates both aspects of program generosity: spending and eligibility. The second measure of Medicaid generosity has the same basic characteristics but focuses specifically on long-term care. In this case, the measure was calculated as state-level Medicaid expenditures on long-term care per poor elderly adult (age 65 and over). The long-term care measure is included in the SVM, whereas the general Medicaid generosity measure is not.

We included the VA labor index in our equations to measure difference in wages across geographic areas. The VA labor index is used to adjust allocations in the current system.

In addition, in the AVM, we included a measure of the average physical condition of the buildings at the facility. It is measured on a scale of one to five, with higher scores indicating better physical condition. These data were taken from the VA's Capital Asset Baseline Assessment.

Also included in the equations are several variables aimed at measuring medical education and research activity related to academic affiliations, based on the findings from our review of the literature (see Wasserman et al., 2001). To assess the impact of teaching on the provision of patient care services by teaching physicians, we constructed a variable based on the ratio of residents to physicians per facility. This variable measures the intensity of physician involvement in teaching activities (that is, the higher the resident to physician ratio, the more involved physicians are in teaching activities) and also accounts for the net impact of residents on physician productivity. Although teaching activities reduce the time that physicians who teach can devote to patient care activities, residents also provide patient care. In addition to the medical education variable, we constructed two variables to measure research intensity. One measured total research costs per 1,000 unique patients; the other measured the percentage of all funded research that took place at each facility.

Data Cleaning and Imputation

In this section, we describe the steps we took to clean and prepare the data for analysis.

Individual Data

In general, the data that were obtained for the patient-level analysis were complete, clean, and deemed reliable. However, for some variables, such as income, missing data were a problem. When possible, we used information from other years or other observations on the same person within the same year to logically impute values for the missing variables. This method was used in cases where the variable value for an individual would be unlikely to change over time (e.g., gender and race) or would change in a predictable fashion (e.g., age).[10] In cases where we were unable to logically impute a value for the variable, we imputed values for individuals using facility-specific means. Specifically, when a person had a missing value for a particular characteristic, we assigned him or her the average value of that charac-

---

[10] For example, if information on gender was missing for an individual in the FY 2001 data, we looked at data for FY 1998, FY 1999, and FY 2000 to see if gender was reported in another year. If data for another year had information on the individual's gender, then we assigned that information to the FY 2001 observation. This sort of logical imputation is particularly useful for variables such as gender that we would not expect to change over time.

teristic for people treated at the same facility. In cases where a person went to more than one facility during the year, we used the average characteristics from the facility at which he or she incurred the most costs. We believed that it was important to impute all missing values, rather than include a missing data category as we did in the Phase II report, so that the model does not reward VISNs that collect less-complete data.[11]

Data on individual-level Medicare expenditures were needed to generate the measure of Medicare reliance used in the patient-level equation. Unfortunately, expenditure information was not available for individuals who are enrolled in Medicare managed-care (Medicare+Choice) plans. However, for such individuals, the data did indicate the number of months the individual was enrolled. We used this information, as well as information on the VA facility (or facilities) where the person was treated, to impute Medicare expenditures for people in Medicare+Choice plans.[12] A timing issue also arises in the calculation of Medicare reliance. The most recent Medicare expenditure data that were available to us were from FY 2000. As such, the FY 2000 data on Medicare expenditures (including the imputed values for the managed-care plan enrollees) were brought forward to use in our cost equations for FY 2001.[13] We inflated the FY 2000 Medicare expenditures into 2001 dollars using the medical care component of the Consumer Price Index to make them comparable with the VA cost data. In addition, we imputed Medicare expenditures for those individuals who were Medicare-eligible (age 65 and over) but for whom we had no Medicare expenditure data in FY 2000.[14] This group consisted primarily of individuals who became Medicare eligible during FY 2001. Because we did not have any information on the number of months the newly eligible were enrolled, we imputed six months of Medicare costs for this group.

Facility Data

The data that were obtained to measure various facility characteristics came from an array of sources within the VA. While most of the data elements were relatively clean and complete, combining the data elements was difficult. The problem stems primarily from recent management consolidations, which led to facility information being reported at different levels in different systems. For example, much of the information on facility infrastructure was measured in FY 2001 and reflected the consolidation of facilities. However, the data on costs and staffing patterns still include information for individual facilities that have since been consolidated.[15] Moreover, the patient-level data include patient treatment information for these facilities. As such, we spent a great deal of time reviewing the facility data and aggregating them (or disaggregating them in some cases) to generate data for a consistent set of facilities.

---

[11] For example, in Phase II we found that having a missing value for rural or urban status was associated with higher costs. In this case, if the VA were to adopt the regression-based allocation approach, VISNs could potentially increase their predicted costs and thus their allocation by not reporting information on patient zip codes (the information used to assign rural or urban status).

[12] The imputation procedure assigns the facility-specific average fee-for-service Medicare expenditure to individuals treated at that VA facility and who were enrolled in Medicare managed-care plans. The average is scaled to reflect the number of months the individual was enrolled in the managed-care plan.

[13] In doing so, we have implicitly assumed that Medicare reliance is stable over time, at least in the short run.

[14] For these imputations, facility-specific average expenditures (based on fee-for-service clients) were assigned to individuals for whom no FY 2000 Medicare information exists.

[15] In most cases, the consolidation reflects only a change in management organization and does not indicate that the consolidated facility has been closed.

In cases where facilities were missing some data elements, we assigned the median value for that variable across all facilities.

Statistical Techniques

The overall goal of the analyses was to evaluate the potential impact on health care costs of various patient- and facility-level characteristics. As indicated above, to this end, we estimated the following multivariate equation of annual VA health care costs:[16]

$$C_i = X_i'\beta_1 + H_i'\beta_2 + A_i'\beta_3 + L_i'\beta_4 + W_i'\beta_5 + \varepsilon_i, \qquad (2.1)$$

where

C_i is equal to the total annual costs for veteran i;

X_i is a vector of sociodemographic variables for veteran i;

H_i is a vector of health status (or case mix) variables for veteran i;

A_i is a vector of availability of local health care resources (that is, physicians and hospital beds) for veteran i;

L_i is a vector of geographic location variables for veteran i;

W_i is a vector of VA facility characteristics where veteran i was treated;

ε_i is an error term that is independently and identically distributed (i.i.d.)$(0,\sigma^2)$; and

$\beta_1 - \beta_5$ are vectors of parameters to be estimated.

In general, annual health care cost data have a very skewed distribution (i.e., a large number of patients with low costs and a long right tail representing the small number of patients with very high costs), and the VA data are no exception. When this skewness occurs, standard linear regression using the dollar value of annual costs as the dependent variable may not fit the data very well. As an alternative, researchers often use alternative specifications such as ordinary least squares (OLS) regression with a log or square root transformation of the dependent variable or gamma regression with a log link (Manning and Mullahy, 2001).

However, for the present analyses, we chose to use standard OLS regression models in the interests of simplicity, transparency, and consistency.[17] One of the goals of the VERA system is for the allocation framework to be simple and predictable. We have developed our

---

[16] To generate robust standard errors for the estimates, the analysis was clustered at the facility level. Clustering accounts for the possibility that the observations for people treated within the same facility are not statistically independent of each other.

[17] We recognize that a trade-off may exist between transparency/simplicity and selecting the functional form for the regression equations that provides the best "fit." However, a paper by Wagner, Chen, and Barnett (2003) supports our choice to use the linear model. Using data on veterans age 65 and over, they found that while the log transformation helped reduce the appearance of skewness, the OLS model consistently performed better than models with logged cost-adjusted charges as the dependent variable. They found, for instance, that when they compared the OLS and semi-log models, the OLS model had substantially lower absolute mean error. Citing an article by Lipscomb and colleagues, they argued that the ability to predict costs should be the primary concern when choosing the appropriate statistical model. This argument is particularly relevant given one of the main objectives of our study, that is, to aggregate predicted costs and assess how VISN allocations should change.

analytic strategy with this goal in mind. Models with log or square root transformations and gamma regressions are more complicated than the linear model, and the results from these specifications are more difficult to interpret. Moreover, the linear specification is used in much of the existing literature on risk adjustment. This consistency with the previous literature is desirable because it provides the context for the interpretation of our results. In addition, the truncation of total costs at $70,000 to reflect the high-cost patient adjustments that are currently made under VERA eliminates many of the extreme outliers, making the standard OLS estimation more appropriate.

The estimates from the regression equations identify the factors, both patient level and facility level, that have a significant influence on costs. However, these estimates do not directly address the question of how VISN allocations would be changed if these variables were considered in VERA. To address this question, we used the regression estimates to simulate VERA allocations to VISNs under various scenarios.

The first step in the simulation process was to generate predicted annual costs for each patient, using Equation 2.1. It is important to note that the predictions are based only on the variables included in the equation. Thus, unobserved factors such as efficiency and quality of care are not directly taken into account.[18]

The second step in the simulation process involved aggregating the predicted patient-level costs to the VISN level. Because some veterans incur costs in multiple VISNs during the year, we distributed each individual's annual predicted cost across facilities based on the share of actual costs that were incurred by that individual at each facility. This allowed predicted costs to be aggregated to the facility and VISN levels. The VISN-level aggregate can be interpreted as an estimate of the costs the VISN would be expected to incur based on the characteristics of the individuals they treat and the characteristics of their facilities.

The VISN-level predicted costs could then be used to generate a simulated allocation for any lump-sum appropriation. To do this, we used the VISN-level predicted costs to calculate the proportion of total predicted costs incurred by each VISN. The share estimates can then be applied to any given appropriation to derive the associated VISN-level VERA allocations. The calculation of the simulated allocation for a particular VISN is illustrated in Equation 2.2.

$$\text{Allocation for VISN}_i = \frac{\text{Predicted Cost for VISN}_i}{\sum_{i=1}^{22} \text{Predicted Cost for VISN}_i} * \left(\text{Appropriation}\right). \quad (2.2)$$

We applied this allocation share, as calculated above, to the total FY 2003 health care appropriation, less the high-cost patient adjustments, to obtain allocations for each VISN. We then added in the actual high-cost adjustment that each VISN received in FY 2003 to obtain final allocations that distribute the total FY 2003 health care appropriation.

To interpret the simulation results, it is useful to have a basis of comparison, or benchmark allocation, against which each simulation can be judged. The actual FY 2003 al-

---

[18] However, if variables that are omitted from the regression are correlated with both the dependent variable and one or more of the included covariates, the estimated coefficients for the included covariates will be biased. In other words, the coefficient estimates will pick up some of the effects of the excluded variables. As such, the SVM may indirectly take into account some characteristics not included in the model.

location is perhaps the most obvious benchmark. However, the comparison between the simulated allocations and the actual FY 2003 allocations confounds two different effects: (1) the difference in methodology (regression versus workload counts and national prices) for determining the allocations and (2) the difference in the patient- and facility-level characteristics that are included in the models. In an effort to separate out these two effects, we made three additional comparisons.

First, we used the results from the BRM to simulate a base case allocation for each VISN. Because the BRM includes only variables that are used in the current VERA system, the comparison between the base case and actual FY 2003 allocations isolates the difference that is due to the methodology used.

The second type of comparison we made was between the simulated allocations from the BRM and the simulated allocations from the SVM with VERA-10. These comparisons show the impact of the additional patient and facility variables that we controlled for in our regression equations, using the same case-mix variables.

The third type of comparison was designed to isolate the effect of using an alternative case-mix measure, VA DCGs, on VISN allocations. Here we compared the VERA-10 SVM simulations with those based on the VA DCGs case-mix specifications. Since the case-mix measure that is used represents the only difference among these models, the results of these comparisons illustrate the effect of the alternative case-mix measure on VISN allocations.

Disaggregation Analyses

In addition to using the models described above to simulate VISN allocations, we disaggregated the simulated results by each of the variables included in the models. Doing so sheds light on why each VISN gains or loses simulated revenue. Toward this end, we compared each VISN's simulated allocations, under the various models described above, with what each network would have received if the network's patients and facilities had the national average values for all of the variables included in the models.[19] We refer to this new figure as the *unadjusted average allocation* (this is essentially a workload-based allocation where each VISN gets a specified amount per person treated).

We then calculated the dollar value of the difference between a given simulated allocation (e.g., using the SVM) and the unadjusted average allocation. This comparison provides information on the total effect of adjusting for each variable in the model of interest (e.g., the SVM). The total effect can be disaggregated to identify the effect of each variable included in the model. This disaggregation is accomplished by sequentially setting each variable equal to the actual value and calculating the difference in a given VISN's allocation between what it would receive under the simulated allocation when the variable assumes its actual value and what the network would receive when the variable is set to the national average value (the unadjusted average allocation). For example, consider the analysis for the health status measure. The difference between the unadjusted average allocation and the allocation when all characteristics except health status are set to the national average indicates whether a VISN will receive more or less money once health status is considered. If a VISN has patients that are sicker than the national average, the VISN will receive a higher alloca-

---

[19] Note that for categorical variables, we assumed that the VISN would have the national distribution for those variables.

tion when health status is considered. Similarly, if a VISN has healthier-than-average patients, accounting for health status will reduce the network's allocation below the unadjusted average allocation.

CHAPTER THREE

Results

This chapter presents the results of the analyses described in Chapter Two. Specifically, we discuss findings related to our regression equations, which measured the influence of various patient and facility characteristics on the costs of caring for patients at VA hospitals and clinics. In addition, this chapter presents the results of simulations, based on the regression models, of how VISN allocations would change if the VA adopted a regression-based approach to determine such allocations and considered additional factors that affect patient care costs. Finally, the simulated allocations are disaggregated to provide a better understanding of the effect of each variable included in the regression model. Throughout the chapter, we have focused our discussion on the set of results that we believe to be most relevant for policy purposes, the SVM. Complete findings from the regression, simulation, and disaggregation analyses are contained in Appendix C.

Model Specification Test

We began the analysis by constructing a set of patient- and facility-level regression equations similar to those used in the Phase II analysis. We used this two-equation model to identify the variables to be included in the SVM. Once the variables were selected, we chose to simplify the modeling approach by collapsing the patient- and facility-level equations into a single equation. To compare the results from the two different specifications, we calculated the mean squared prediction error (MSPE)—a measure of how well the model predicts—for each model.[1] The specification test revealed that the single-equation and the two-equation modeling approaches performed almost identically (MSPE = 7,403 for the single-equation model and MSPE = 7,410 for the two-equation model). Therefore, we chose to continue with the simpler approach and will present results only from the single-equation model.

Regression Results

We restricted the primary analysis sample to those veterans who are included in the workload count in the current VERA allocation methodology; that is, we excluded Priority 7 veterans

---

[1] To calculate the MSPE, we first calculated the prediction error for each individual patient in the sample (i.e., predicted total costs from the model minus actual total costs) and squared it (prediction error × prediction error). We then took the average of the squared prediction errors across all of the individuals in the sample to arrive at the MSPE.

who are in the Basic Care patient categories and patients who are not veterans, such as non-veteran employees. The final sample for FY 2001 includes 3,186,221 veterans.

Descriptive statistics are presented in Table 3.1. Approximately 46 percent of the sample is 65 years of age or older, 95 percent is male, 55 percent is married, 24 percent is a racial/ethnic minority, 73 percent lives in urban areas, and 57 percent reported an annual

Table 3.1
Descriptive Statistics for Patient- and Facility-Level Variables

Variable Category		Mean	Std Dev
Patient-level variables			
Age			
	Less than 25	0.008	0.086
	25–34	0.042	0.199
	35–44	0.091	0.286
	45–54	0.221	0.412
	55–64	0.173	0.376
	65–74	0.230	0.418
	75–84	0.212	0.406
	85 and over	0.023	0.148
Income			
	Missing	0.126	0.332
	$20,000 or less	0.572	0.495
	$21,000–$40,000	0.237	0.425
	$41,000–$60,000	0.038	0.191
	$61,000–$80,000	0.012	0.111
	More than $80,000	0.015	0.122
Race			
	Hispanic	0.055	0.200
	American Indian	0.004	0.049
	Black	0.179	0.319
	Asian	0.007	0.071
	White	0.755	0.361
Gender			
	Female	0.049	0.216
	Male	0.951	0.216
Marital status			
	Single	0.446	0.486
	Married	0.554	0.486
Physicians per capita			
	Less than 0.001	0.259	0.438
	0.001 to 0.002	0.250	0.433
	0.0021 to 0.003	0.243	0.429
	Greater than 0.003	0.248	0.432
Hospital beds per capita			
	Less than 0.003	0.419	0.493
	0.003 to 0.006	0.482	0.500
	Greater than 0.006	0.099	0.299
Rural or urban status of patient's residence			
	Urban	0.726	0.444
	Suburban	0.161	0.366
	Rural	0.069	0.252
	Very rural	0.044	0.205
Distance to closest facility		46.531	49.690
Distance to closest CBOC		23.033	21.662
Priority Group			
	1	0.155	0.362
	2	0.087	0.282
	3	0.151	0.358
	4	0.049	0.215
	5	0.478	0.500
	6	0.009	0.097
	7	0.070	0.256

Table 3.1—continued

Variable Category		Mean	Std Dev
Medicare reliance			
	Not eligible	0.543	0.498
	No reliance	0.146	0.353
	FFS—1 to 24%	0.091	0.288
	FFS—25 to 49%	0.043	0.202
	FFS—50 to 75%	0.043	0.203
	FFS—75 to 100%	0.072	0.258
	HMO—1 to 24%	0.002	0.047
	HMO—25 to 49%	0.005	0.073
	HMO—50 to 75%	0.014	0.118
	HMO—75 to 100%	0.041	0.198
Medicaid generosity (general)		3739.167	1971.638
Medicaid generosity for LTC		7222.451	3844.380
Facility-level variables			
Rural or urban status of facility			
	Urban	0.915	0.272
	Suburban	0.063	0.238
	Rural	0.015	0.119
	Very rural	0.005	0.070
Residents per full-time MD		0.720	0.485
VA labor index		99.631	4.026
Average food cost per bed day		6.424	2.938
Energy price (dollars per million Btus)		8.715	1.317
Contract labor costs (percentage of total labor costs)		5.437	2.663
Square feet of building space per acre of land		20.396	27.433
Square feet of building space per unique patient		32.972	16.226
Research costs per 1,000 unique patients		71.000	80.740
Percentage of funded research		0.010	0.012
Average building age as of 2001		40.316	15.070
Average building condition (scale of 1–5)		3.308	0.578
Leased square feet per patient		1.187	1.220
Ratio of historic to total number of buildings		0.198	0.225
Total number of buildings		43.804	39.516
Indicator for recent facility/management consolidation		0.261	0.434
Occupancy rate		0.819	0.238
Number of CBOCs per 1,000 unique patients		0.139	0.096
Direct patient care FTEs per 1,000 unique patients		9.117	2.900
Non-patient care FTEs per 1,000 unique patients		29.763	9.655
LTC beds per 1,000 unique patients		4.593	5.317
Special program beds per 1,000 unique patients		0.292	0.607

NOTE: N = 3,186,221.

income of $20,000 or less. However, the income data must be interpreted with caution because the data are based on voluntary self-reports and are missing for 13 percent of the sample. A plurality of veterans (48 percent) is in Priority Group 5. Priority Groups 1 and 3 are the second and third largest groups, each constituting about 15 percent of the sample. Priority Group 7 is relatively small because our sample includes only those Priority 7 veterans who are currently included in VERA workload estimates.

The descriptive statistics illustrate some of the issues associated with the measurement and imputation of Medicare reliance at the patient level. Approximately 54 percent of the sample is not eligible for Medicare, primarily because of age requirements. Slightly over 6 percent of the sample is enrolled in Medicare health maintenance organizations (HMOs), the group for which we had to impute Medicare costs. The remainder of the sample is split between Medicare eligibles who did not use any Medicare services during the past year (15 percent) and people enrolled in Medicare fee-for-service (FFS) plans (25 percent).

For the facility variables, the descriptive results show that a large majority of people were treated at facilities in urban areas (92 percent). With respect to infrastructure, on average, patients were treated at facilities that have 44 buildings with an average age of 40 years. Moreover, the buildings are in average physical condition (average score of 3.3 on a scale of 1 to 5 with 5 being the best), and 20 percent have historical significance. The scope of management consolidations is evident in that more than one-quarter of patients were treated at a facility that had recently undergone a consolidation.

We have also tabulated descriptive statistics at the VISN level, which are shown in Appendix B. Because many of the patient- and facility-level variables used in the analysis differ across VISNs, we believed it was important to include a reference table of VISN-level descriptive statistics in the report. Table B.1 provides a context for understanding the simulation results described later in this chapter.

Table 3.2 shows the proportion of variation (i.e., R-squared statistics) in annual VA patient care costs that is explained by each of the regression equations, ranging from a low of 0.46 for the BRM to a high of 0.62 in the SVM with VA DCGs as the case-mix measure. We recognize that maximizing the explanatory power of the regression equation is not necessarily the only goal of policymakers; other factors, such as simplicity, transparency, stability, and acceptability, are also important. These issues informed our selection of the variables included in the SVM and ultimately our conclusions, as described in Chapter Four.

Parameter estimates and t-statistics from each of the three regression equations are presented in Table 3.2. Most parameter estimates are statistically distinguishable from zero at $p < 0.05$, a result that is not surprising given the very large sample size. Although the model is estimated as a single equation, we discuss the effects of the patient variables included in the model separately from the effects of the facility-level variables.

Patient Characteristics

Many of the patient characteristics included in the model were defined as categorical variables. When a set of mutually exclusive categorical variables is used in a regression, the indicator for one of the categories must be excluded as a reference. Thus, with respect to the results in Table 3.2, the coefficients on the categorical variables must be interpreted in reference to the category that was excluded from the equation. Taking the effect of age on cost as an example, the equation includes indicators for the age range of the individual (< 25, 25 to 34, 35 to 44, 45 to 54, 55 to 64, 65 to 74, 75 to 84, > 85). In this case, the reference category consists of people under age 25. As a result, the coefficients on the other age indicators are interpreted as the relative cost difference between that particular group and the under-25 age group. Thus, for example, a positive coefficient on the 35–44 age group indicates that this group is more costly to treat than the group of patients under 25 years of age, after controlling for the effects of all the other factors in the regression model. Similarly, a negative coefficient would indicate that a group is less costly than the reference group. The reference category for each set of categorical variables is noted in Table 3.2.

We find the same basic relationship between age and VA patient-care costs across the two different case-mix specifications (SVM with VERA-10 and SVM with VA DCGs). After controlling for all of the other patient and facility characteristics, health care costs appear to

Table 3.2
Selected Variables Regression Models

Variable Category		Base Regression Model (VERA-10) 0.46[a]		Selected Variables Model with VERA-10 0.49[a]		Selected Variables Model with VA DCGs 0.62[a]	
		Estimate	t-Statistic	Estimate	t-Statistic	Estimate	t-Statistic
Intercept		-3682.89	-2.56 *	-4529.14	-3.34 **	-4258.98	-2.90 **
Patient characteristics							
Age	Less than 25			Reference		Reference	
	25–34			47.37	1.30	79.17	1.93
	35–44			536.52	11.91 **	310.97	5.98 **
	45–54			1138.10	24.50 **	625.82	13.30 **
	55–64			1664.95	27.68 **	818.03	15.82 **
	65–74			921.40	15.32 **	311.02	5.49 **
	75–84			976.41	15.03 **	116.62	1.89
	85 and over			965.45	10.83 **	-242.94	-3.05 **
Gender	Female			624.21	15.35 **	604.21	16.22 **
	Male			Reference		Reference	
Physicians per capita	Less than 0.001			-263.85	-3.21 **	-82.69	-1.06
	0.001 to 0.002			-232.83	-3.03 **	-72.21	-0.99
	0.0021 to 0.003			-10.24	-0.12	35.77	0.48
	Greater than 0.003			Reference		Reference	
Hospital beds per capita	Less than 0.003			-245.73	-3.27 **	-168.50	-2.20 *
	0.003 to 0.006			-224.86	-3.41 **	-125.94	-1.80
	Greater than 0.006			Reference		Reference	
Rural or urban status	Urban			154.54	1.78	130.93	1.87
	Suburban			7.55	0.12	29.77	0.54
	Rural			-53.92	-1.06	-64.74	-1.39
	Very rural			Reference		Reference	
Distance to closest facility				1.97	2.17 *	2.39	3.27 **
Distance to closest CBOC				5.82	3.66 **	2.44	1.65 *
Medicare reliance	Not eligible			Reference		Reference	
	No reliance			2260.80	33.56 **	1236.20	26.90 **
	FFS—1 to 24%			3684.21	39.12 **	1946.59	34.50 **
	FFS—25 to 49%			686.78	13.03 **	42.07	1.03
	FFS—50 to 74%			-265.07	-4.90 **	-550.06	-11.40 **

Table 3.2—continued

Variable Category	Base Regression Model (VERA-10) 0.46[a]		Selected Variables Model with VERA-10 0.49[a]		Selected Variables Model with VA DCGs 0.62[a]	
	Estimate	t-Statistic	Estimate	t-Statistic	Estimate	t-Statistic
FFS—75 to 100%			-1322.35	-19.94 **	-1011.27	-21.38 **
HMO—1 to 24%			23904.81	34.19 **	17481.95	22.61 **
HMO—25 to 49%			6994.76	19.45 **	3198.12	10.61 **
HMO—50 to 74%			1124.86	10.87 **	181.48	1.88
HMO—75 to 100%			-1346.43	-16.29 **	-743.69	-11.30 **
Medicaid generosity for LTC			0.004	0.30	0.01	0.82
VERA-10 patient category						
1	Reference		Reference			
2	2,073.32	34.03 **	1,385.90	27.55 **		
3	3,292.75	42.28 **	2,414.60	34.98 **		
4	3,125.87	31.50 **	2,246.97	30.40 **		
5	6,735.25	42.16 **	5,648.56	42.13 **		
6	15,469.82	58.37 **	13,630.58	58.20 **		
7	15,846.65	52.69 **	14,114.18	51.20 **		
8	22,507.05	53.06 **	20,288.13	52.20 **		
9	29,631.93	49.93 **	27,627.07	47.27 **		
10	53,377.39	112.02 **	50,087.41	113.56 **		
VA DCG patient category						
DCG 0.1					Reference	
DCG 0.2					423.01	24.74 **
DCG 0.3					771.13	34.65 **
DCG 0.4					522.22	21.67 **
DCG 0.5					921.83	34.67 **
DCG 0.7					1,009.69	38.40 **
DCG 1					1,541.71	43.34 **
DCG 1.5					2,055.98	45.91 **
DCG 2					2,480.45	43.99 **
DCG 2.5					2,730.54	45.06 **
DCG 3					3,563.89	44.41 **
DCG 4					4,565.04	40.94 **
DCG 5					5,858.75	45.09 **
DCG 6					8,222.71	50.62 **
DCG 7.5					12,608.38	54.00 **

Note — VERA-10 patient categories: 1 Non-Reliant, 2 Basic Medical, 3 Mental Health, 4 Heart, Lung, and GI, 5 Oncology, 6 Multiple Problem, 7 Specialized Care, 8 Supportive Care, 9 Chronic Mental Illness, 10 Critically Ill.

Table 3.2—continued

Variable Category	Base Regression Model (VERA-10)[a] 0.46[a]		Selected Variables Model with VERA-10[a] 0.49[a]		Selected Variables Model with VA DCGs[a] 0.62[a]	
	Estimate	t-Statistic	Estimate	t-Statistic	Estimate	t-Statistic
DCG 10					22,894.69	67.89 **
DCG 15					35,120.61	73.43 **
DCG 20					42,000.18	84.14 **
DCG 25					47,954.51	98.50 **
DCG 30					53,924.57	115.63 **
DCG 40					60,429.57	150.06 **
DCG 50					62,504.48	121.50 **
DCG 60					64,840.69	142.54 **
DCG 70					65,119.75	106.95 **
Facility characteristics						
Rural or urban status of facility						
Urban			22.26	0.09	−215.08	−0.79
Suburban			−280.31	−1.20	−504.63	−1.81
Rural			−334.00	−1.13	−419.35	−1.32
Very rural			Reference		Reference	
Residents per full-time MD	432.91	3.63 **	226.34	2.39 *	−75.72	−0.83
VA labor index	35.41	2.46 *	33.15	2.31 *	38.77	2.57 *
Average food cost per bed day			20.06	1.26	5.34	0.34
Energy price (dollars per million Btus)			−7.54	−0.27	22.77	0.73
Contract labor costs			−5.88	−0.35	3.46	0.20
Square feet of building space per acre of land			2.58	1.67	4.17	3.89 **
Square feet of building space per unique patient			9.53	2.94 **	10.83	2.76 **
Research costs per unique patient	4.07	5.76 **	3.94	5.87 **	4.06	5.67 **

NOTE: * indicates significance at the 95% level and ** at the 99% level. Robust t-statistics are calculated by clustering data at the facility level.
[a] R-squared.

increase with age until age 65. At that point, the costs begin to decline (after controlling for Medicare reliance and other factors). In fact, in the SVM with VA DCGs, we find that, all other things being equal, the veterans over 85 actually use fewer resources than the under-25 age group (the reference group). This finding may reflect in part the fact that high-cost outliers are truncated at $70,000 and that the oldest veterans are more likely to be included in this group.

A patient's health status has an important influence on the costs he or she incurs. Consequently, the case-mix variables included in each of the equations are typically highly statistically significant and behave as expected, with higher resource use found among patients in higher case-mix categories (i.e., patients who are sicker use more resources).

We found that, in addition to age, another basic demographic variable, gender, plays an important role in explaining health care costs. More precisely, across the two case-mix specifications, VA patient care costs are higher for women than for men. By comparison, previous non-VA studies indicate that young women have higher costs than young men, whereas elderly women have lower costs than do elderly men (Ash et al., 2000; Pope et al., 2000).

The coefficient estimates on the measures of the supply of other health care resources in the area indicate that health care market characteristics may be important. In the SVM with VERA-10, veterans living in areas with a greater concentration of physicians and hospital beds, a general characteristic of urban areas, tend to have higher VA patient care costs. Although the estimates from the SVM with VA DCGs tell a similar story, they are not statistically significant.

Surprisingly, an individual's use of VA resources tends to increase as his or her distance to the VA health care facility increases. This finding is inconsistent with previous research showing that use of a medical service tends to decrease with a corresponding increase in distance between the beneficiary and the provider of the service (see, e.g., Shannon, Skinner, and Bashshur, 1973; Weiss, Greenlick, and Jones, 1970; Cohen and Lee, 1985; and Shannon, Bashshur, and Lovett, 1986).

The measure of reliance on Medicare has the expected influence: Veterans who are more reliant on Medicare use fewer VA resources than do other veterans. The results also suggest that the magnitude of the effect of Medicare reliance depends on the type of Medicare plan in which the veteran is enrolled. Veterans who are in Medicare managed care plans appear to use more VA resources than do veterans enrolled in standard fee-for-service plans. However, it is important to note that because we had to impute values for Medicare HMO enrollees, there is the potential for measurement error in this variable. In contrast to the results for Medicare reliance, we find no effect of state-level Medicaid generosity on individual health care costs.

Although the direction (sign) and significance of the coefficient estimates on the patient-level characteristics are relatively similar across the case-mix specifications, the magnitudes vary. In general, the coefficient estimates on the demographic characteristics from the SVM with the VA DCGs equation are smaller in absolute value than the estimates from the SVM with the VERA-10 equation. This result indicates that the VA DCGs case-mix measure, because it is more refined, picks up differences in health status that were being reflected in other variables, such as age, under the VA patient classification-based case-mix measures (i.e., VERA-10).

Facility Characteristics

We found that only a few facility-level characteristics had a significant impact on patient health care costs across both case-mix specifications, including the VISN labor index, research costs per patient, and square feet of building space per patient. In contrast, for two variables in the SVM, the significance of the association with costs depends on which health status measure is included in the model. For example, under the SVM with VERA-10, the number of residents per full-time physician has a positive effect on patient costs—that is, they increase costs—but is insignificant in the model with VA DCGs. Along the same lines, we find that the square feet of building space per acre of land is positively related to increased costs in the SVM with VA DCGs, but the relationship is insignificant in the model with VERA-10 used as the measure of health status.

The differences across the two specifications likely reflect differences in what the health status variables are measuring. As noted in Chapter Two, the VERA-10 and VA DCGs case-mix measures are constructed in very different ways using different types of information. In general, the VA DCGs measure of health status is more detailed; it contains 25 patient groups and does a better job of explaining variation in costs across patients. The difference in the direction of the effect of residents per full-time physician between the SVM with VERA-10 and the model with VA DCGs serves to highlight some of the differences in the two case-mix measures. Under the SVM with VERA-10, we find that having more residents per physician increases costs. However, when VA DCGs are used to control for health status, we find the opposite: More residents per physician can actually increase productivity. The positive effect on costs found under the model with VERA-10 can be explained by the fact that the facilities that tend to have more residents are generally the larger tertiary care centers, which also tend to treat the sickest and most expensive patients. Thus, the less we control for health status, the more likely we are to find a positive association between the number of residents and patient costs. That the positive effect disappears and actually turns negative when the VA DCGs case-mix measure is used is further evidence that the VA DCGs measure controls more fully for differences in health status across individuals.

Simulation Results

The results from the BRM and SVM regression models were used to simulate VISN allocations.[2] To interpret the simulation results, we made three types of comparisons.

First, we compared the actual FY 2003 VERA allocations and the simulated VERA allocations from the BRM. These are the allocations our regression-based methodology would yield when taking into account only those variables—the VERA-10 patient categories, the labor index, research costs, and teaching costs—that are currently incorporated into VERA. This comparison allowed us to isolate the effect of the difference between our regression-based methodology and the VERA methodology currently used by the VA.

Second, we compared our SVM with VERA-10 simulated allocations and the allocations from the BRM. This comparison allowed us to determine the effects of the additional variables included in the SVM, holding the methodology constant.

---

[2] Simulation results based on the AVM are contained in Appendix C.

Finally, we compared simulated allocations from the SVM with VERA-10 and those from the SVM with VA DCGs to isolate the effect of alternative health status measures. All of the simulated allocations have been normalized to distribute the $20.5 billion appropriation for FY 2003.[3]

Actual Versus Base Case Allocations

In our first comparison, presented in Table 3.3, we find that the simulated allocations from the BRM are quite similar to the actual FY 2003 allocations. While 11 VISNs would obtain a larger allocation under the BRM simulation than they did under the current VERA system, the percentage differences are relatively small, with only one VISN seeing a difference of 5 percent or more. In aggregate, moving to the regression-based methodology would redistribute approximately $159 million, or 0.8 percent of the total appropriation.

Table 3.3
Comparison of Simulated Allocations from the Base Regression Model to Actual FY 2003 Allocations

| | | Base Regression Model | |
VISN	VERA FY 03 Actual Allocation	Simulated Allocation	% diff FY 03
01 Boston	1,012,354	1,026,815	1.4%
02 Albany	556,418	555,058	−0.2%
03 Bronx	1,111,597	1,052,198	−5.3%
04 Pittsburgh	1,076,519	1,090,602	1.3%
05 Baltimore	617,523	619,825	0.4%
06 Durham	990,671	985,498	−0.5%
07 Atlanta	1,158,656	1,159,770	0.1%
08 Bay Pines	1,655,761	1,683,309	1.7%
09 Nashville	926,758	936,261	1.0%
10 Cincinnati	771,274	772,437	0.2%
11 Ann Arbor	849,127	841,891	−0.9%
12 Chicago	978,050	971,537	−0.7%
15 Kansas City	761,453	728,287	−4.4%
16 Jackson	1,688,502	1,660,811	−1.6%
17 Dallas	936,733	935,714	−0.1%
18 Phoenix	803,265	791,490	−1.5%
19 Denver	528,463	522,899	−1.1%
20 Portland	902,764	920,155	1.9%
21 San Francisco	1,062,177	1,079,743	1.7%
22 Long Beach	1,219,641	1,251,681	2.6%
23 Lincoln & Minneapolis	917,822	939,546	2.4%
Total amount redistributed		158,897	
% of FY 03 dollars redistributed		0.8%	

NOTE: Figures shown are in thousands of dollars.

---

[3] The VA medical care appropriation in FY 2003 was $23.9 billion of which $20.5 billion was distributed to the VISNs, as of February 24, 2003, using the VERA model.

The small differences in the results are likely due to three factors. First, we used a regression-based methodology, whereas the current VERA system does not. Second, we measured some variables (e.g., workload and teaching) differently from the way the VA does. Third, our regression methodology is based on one year of data (FY 2001), whereas VERA uses a three-year retrospective to determine Basic Care workload and a five-year retrospective to determine Complex Care workload.

Adding Individual and Facility Variables

In the second set of comparisons, the results are intended to illustrate the effects of adjusting for additional individual and facility characteristics—including demographics, patient location, Medicare reliance, facility infrastructure, and facility location—while holding the regression methodology and case-mix adjustment constant. The overall effect of these adjustments is seen in Table 3.4. In moving from the simulated allocations of the BRM to those of the VERA-10 SVM, 12 VISNs would see an increase in their allocation, whereas the remaining 9 VISNs would see a decrease. However, the magnitude of the changes is relatively

Table 3.4
Comparison of Simulated Allocations from the Selected Variables Model with VERA-10 and the Base Regression Model

VISN	Base Regression Model	Selected Variables Model with VERA-10	
		Simulated Allocation	% diff
01 Boston	1,026,815	1,021,037	−0.6%
02 Albany	555,058	580,827	4.6%
03 Bronx	1,052,198	1,048,717	−0.3%
04 Pittsburgh	1,090,602	1,037,018	−4.9%
05 Baltimore	619,825	611,566	−1.3%
06 Durham	985,498	994,306	0.9%
07 Atlanta	1,159,770	1,167,886	0.7%
08 Bay Pines	1,683,309	1,629,710	−3.2%
09 Nashville	936,261	960,519	2.6%
10 Cincinnati	772,437	743,647	−3.7%
11 Ann Arbor	841,891	850,192	1.0%
12 Chicago	971,537	990,930	2.0%
15 Kansas City	728,287	719,407	−1.2%
16 Jackson	1,660,811	1,708,003	2.8%
17 Dallas	935,714	929,633	−0.6%
18 Phoenix	791,490	794,982	0.4%
19 Denver	522,899	526,247	0.6%
20 Portland	920,155	933,693	1.5%
21 San Francisco	1,079,743	1,093,188	1.2%
22 Long Beach	1,251,681	1,204,542	−3.8%
23 Lincoln & Minneapolis	939,546	979,479	4.3%
Total amount redistributed		215,592	
% of FY 03 dollars redistributed		1.1%	

NOTE: Figures shown are in thousands of dollars.

small, with no VISN seeing a difference (positive or negative) that is as large as 5 percent. Overall, the move from the BRM to the SVM with VERA-10 would redistribute $216 million, or 1.1 percent of the appropriation.

Comparing Alternative Case-Mix Measures

The third type of comparison was designed to illustrate the effect of changing case-mix methodologies on VISN-level allocations. Here, we compared the simulated allocations from the VERA-10 SVM and those from the same model with VA DCGs to isolate the effect of the different case-mix measures. The results of this comparison, presented in Table 3.5, show that 12 VISNs would receive higher and 9 VISNs would receive lower allocations if VA DCGs were used to adjust for case mix rather than VERA-10. The magnitude of the gains and losses, while still relatively small, shows a wider range than was observed in the previous comparisons. For example, the simulated allocation for VISN 19 (Denver) increases by 11.7 percent when moving from the VERA-10 SVM model to the VA DCGs SVM model. At the other end of the spectrum, VISN 4 (Pittsburgh) sees the largest reduction, 6.5 percent, in its

Table 3.5
Comparison of Simulated Allocations from the Selected Variables Models with VA DCGs and with VERA-10

		Selected Variables Model with VA DCGs	
VISN	Selected Variables Model with VERA-10	Simulated Allocation	% diff
01 Boston	1,021,037	993,664	−2.7%
02 Albany	580,827	582,579	0.3%
03 Bronx	1,048,717	1,058,272	0.9%
04 Pittsburgh	1,037,018	969,658	−6.5%
05 Baltimore	611,566	596,833	−2.4%
06 Durham	994,306	964,141	−3.0%
07 Atlanta	1,167,886	1,162,743	−0.4%
08 Bay Pines	1,629,710	1,640,071	0.6%
09 Nashville	960,519	976,477	1.7%
10 Cincinnati	743,647	751,565	1.1%
11 Ann Arbor	850,192	835,871	−1.7%
12 Chicago	990,930	1,004,644	1.4%
15 Kansas City	719,407	748,813	4.1%
16 Jackson	1,708,003	1,676,286	−1.9%
17 Dallas	929,633	901,935	−3.0%
18 Phoenix	794,982	813,545	2.3%
19 Denver	526,247	587,963	11.7%
20 Portland	933,693	975,788	4.5%
21 San Francisco	1,093,188	1,103,342	0.9%
22 Long Beach	1,204,542	1,174,447	−2.5%
23 Lincoln & Minneapolis	979,479	1,006,892	2.8%
Total amount redistributed		248,607	
% of FY 03 dollars redistributed		1.2%	

NOTE: Figures shown are in thousands of dollars.

simulated allocation when VA DCGs are used to control for case mix in place of VERA-10. However, at the national level, the change from VERA-10 to VA DCGs in the SVM would redistribute a relatively small amount, approximately 1.2 percent of the total appropriation. The overall effect of moving from the VERA-10 SVM to the VA DCGs SVM is very similar in magnitude to the overall effect of adjusting for additional variables by moving from the BRM to the VERA-10 SVM.

Comparison of Simulation Results to Fiscal Year 2003 Actual Allocations

To this point, the allocation comparisons that we have discussed were designed to isolate the effects of methodology, additional adjustments, and alternative case-mix measures. However, it is important to consider the full impact of the movement from the current system to the regression-based methodology used in our analysis. Thus, we compared simulated allocations from the BRM, the VERA-10 SVM, and the VA DCGs SVM to the actual FY 2003 allocations. The results of this comparison are presented in Table 3.6. Looking across the bottom two rows of the table shows that relative to the actual FY 2003 allocations (determined by

Table 3.6
Comparison of Simulated Allocations from the Base and Selected Variables Regression Models to Actual FY 2003 Allocations

VISN	VERA FY 03 Actual Allocation	Base Regression Model		Selected Variables Model with VERA-10		Selected Variables Model with VA DCGs	
		Simulated Allocation	% diff FY 03	Simulated Allocation	% diff FY 03	Simulated Allocation	% diff FY 03
01 Boston	1,012,354	1,026,815	1.4%	1,021,037	0.9%	993,664	−1.8%
02 Albany	556,418	555,058	−0.2%	580,827	4.4%	582,579	4.7%
03 Bronx	1,111,597	1,052,198	−5.3%	1,048,717	−5.7%	1,058,272	−4.8%
04 Pittsburgh	1,076,519	1,090,602	1.3%	1,037,018	−3.7%	969,658	−9.9%
05 Baltimore	617,523	619,825	0.4%	611,566	−1.0%	596,833	−3.4%
06 Durham	990,671	985,498	−0.5%	994,306	0.4%	964,141	−2.7%
07 Atlanta	1,158,656	1,159,770	0.1%	1,167,886	0.8%	1,162,743	0.4%
08 Bay Pines	1,655,761	1,683,309	1.7%	1,629,710	−1.6%	1,640,071	−0.9%
09 Nashville	926,758	936,261	1.0%	960,519	3.6%	976,477	5.4%
10 Cincinnati	771,274	772,437	0.2%	743,647	−3.6%	751,565	−2.6%
11 Ann Arbor	849,127	841,891	−0.9%	850,192	0.1%	835,871	−1.6%
12 Chicago	978,050	971,537	−0.7%	990,930	1.3%	1,004,644	2.7%
15 Kansas City	761,453	728,287	−4.4%	719,407	−5.5%	748,813	−1.7%
16 Jackson	1,688,502	1,660,811	−1.6%	1,708,003	1.2%	1,676,286	−0.7%
17 Dallas	936,733	935,714	−0.1%	929,633	−0.8%	901,935	−3.7%
18 Phoenix	803,265	791,490	−1.5%	794,982	−1.0%	813,545	1.3%
19 Denver	528,463	522,899	−1.1%	526,247	−0.4%	587,963	11.3%
20 Portland	902,764	920,155	1.9%	933,693	3.4%	975,788	8.1%
21 San Francisco	1,062,177	1,079,743	1.7%	1,093,188	2.9%	1,103,342	3.9%
22 Long Beach	1,219,641	1,251,681	2.6%	1,204,542	−1.2%	1,174,447	−3.7%
23 Lincoln & Minneapolis	917,822	939,546	2.4%	979,479	6.7%	1,006,892	9.7%
Total amount redistributed		158,897		236,760		379,600	
% of FY 03 dollars redistributed		0.8%		1.2%		1.8%	

NOTE: Figures shown are in thousands of dollars.

the current VERA system), the SVM with VA DCGs would redistribute more money ($380 million) than the SVM with VERA-10 ($237 million). Moreover, at the VISN level, we find that some VISNs gain or lose a substantial amount relative to their actual FY 2003 allocation.

It is also interesting to note that there are differences in the direction of the redistribution across the two case-mix measures for six VISNs. In other words, under the VERA-10 SVM, four VISNs would receive an allocation that is greater than the actual FY 2003 allocation (positive percentage change in sixth column of Table 3.6), but under the VA DCGs SVM, those four VISNs would receive an allocation that is smaller than the actual (negative percentage change in last column of Table 3.6). For two other VISNs, the opposite is true: They experience a negative percentage change relative to actual allocations under the SVM with VERA-10 and a positive percentage change relative to actual allocations under the model with VA DCGs. As noted previously, the two case-mix measures considered here are constructed in different ways using different types of information. Therefore, it is not surprising that the two measures have different effects on simulated allocations. We explore these differences further in the next section of the report, where we present the disaggregation of the simulated allocations into effects of each variable included in the SVM for each VISN.

Disaggregation of Simulated Allocations

The results of the disaggregation analysis are presented in Table 3.7 for the VERA-10 SVM and in Table 3.8 for the VA DCGs SVM. The results provided in these tables can be viewed from two different perspectives: the VISN level and the national level.

The VISN-Level View

The first approach is to take a VISN-level perspective and focus on the columns of the table. Looking across the first row of Table 3.7, for example, we see the simulated allocations from the VERA-10 SVM (same as shown in column five of Table 3.6). In the second row, the unadjusted average allocation is presented for each VISN. As noted previously, this allocation can be considered a workload-based allocation because every person is assigned the average value in the simulation. The difference between the simulated allocation from the SVM with VERA-10 and the unadjusted average allocation is shown in the third row of the table. This difference is then disaggregated into the pieces associated with each variable in the model. This breakdown is presented in rows 4 through 22 of Table 3.7. These numbers represent the difference between the unadjusted average allocation and the simulated allocation where the variable of interest takes its actual value, thus providing information on the effect of that specific variable on the VISN's overall allocation. For example, looking across row 13 of the table, we see that VISN 1 receives an additional $29 million dollars over and above the unadjusted average allocation when the simulation uses the actual case mix of the patients treated. This finding suggests that the patients in VISN 1 are, on average, sicker than the general population of people treated at the VA, based on the VERA-10 measure of health status. Similarly, the negative number found for VISN 18 suggests that the population this network treats is generally healthier than average, based on the VERA-10 health status measure. It is important to keep in mind that the interpretation of these differentials depends crucially on the coefficients in the regression model. In the case of health status, the regression model indicated that sicker patients have higher costs. Therefore, a positive differential in row 13 indicates that a VISN has sicker than average, and thus, more costly, patients to treat.

Looking down the column for a particular VISN, one sees that the difference between the unadjusted average allocation and the simulated allocation from the SVM (presented in row 3 of the table) is disaggregated into separate pieces for each variable included in the model. Thus, the difference presented in the third row of the table is equal to the sum of the differentials for each variable, which is shown in the last row of the table. Therefore, for each VISN, the table shows how each variable helps to move the VISN from the unadjusted average, or workload-based, allocation to the simulated allocations from the VERA-10 SVM, in Table 3.7, or the VA DCGs SVM, in Table 3.8.

The National View

The second way to think about the disaggregation results is to take a national perspective and focus on the rows of the tables. The rows provide important information at the national level about which variables have the greatest overall impact on allocations. Looking across the rows of Tables 3.7 and 3.8, we can determine the amount of money redistributed by moving from the unadjusted average allocation to one where the characteristics of interest (e.g., health status) take their actual value. The results of this analysis are summarized in Table 3.9. In general, there is a great deal of correspondence across case-mix specifications in terms of which variables appear to move the most money around. In fact, the five variables that move the most money around are the same, regardless of which case-mix measure is included in the model, although the order differs slightly between measures: health status, research costs per 1,000 unique patients, the VA labor index, Medicare reliance, and the square feet of building space per unique patient. In both case-mix specifications, the amount of money redistributed by the health status measure far exceeds the amount redistributed by any other variable. It is important to note here that the current VA system already adjusts for the top three money movers: health status, research costs, and geographic differences in labor costs.

Table 3.7
Disaggregation of Simulated Allocations from the Selected Variables Model with VERA-10

	VISN 1	VISN 2	VISN 3	VISN 4	VISN 5	VISN 6	VISN 7	VISN 8
(1) Simulated allocations from SVM with VERA-10	1,021,037	580,827	1,048,717	1,037,018	611,566	994,306	1,167,886	1,629,710
(2) Unadjusted average allocation	947,153	567,019	917,287	1,131,336	544,274	1,021,624	1,231,463	1,874,403
(3) Difference (1)–(2)	73,884	13,808	131,429	–94,318	67,291	–27,318	–63,577	–244,693
Patient characteristics								
(4) Age	554	–2,284	–357	444	–2,346	–1,499	–1,348	3,235
(5) Gender	–812	–329	–1,899	–1,594	790	1,435	1,607	–442
(6) Physicians per capita	10,069	297	15,330	1,374	4,122	–9,314	–6,751	2,269
(7) Hospital beds per capita	–2,483	–165	–21	2,371	3,352	149	1,884	2,131
(8) Rural or urban status	1,011	318	6,417	1,853	2,146	–1,928	–2,070	8,343
(9) Distance to closest facility	–5,201	3,619	–8,999	–7,867	–4,403	–2,405	1,040	84
(10) Distance to closest CBOC	–9,333	–7,355	–15,735	–11,069	–7,891	18,551	11,613	–15,775
(11) Medicare reliance	7,499	12,552	–18,440	–36,323	–2,204	3,975	–9,438	–24,992
(12) Medicaid generosity for LTC	3,863	2,171	2,641	3,076	–691	–2,097	–2,295	–3,107
(13) VERA-10 health status measure	29,125	15,623	84,950	–4,853	51,066	13,315	–46,072	–62,442
Facility characteristics								
(14) Rural or urban status	–8,670	2,564	3,744	392	2,402	1,480	479	8,654
(15) Residents per full-time MD	–113	–786	410	–5,691	–94	–6,176	1,047	–15,137
(16) VA labor index	15,733	–6,097	40,419	–2,542	12,164	–12,891	–15,015	–52,159
(17) Average food cost per bed day	302	–7,035	–4,106	–819	–336	–1,624	–1,117	–403
(18) Energy price ($/million Btus)	–1,878	–1,016	–1,138	–24	–1,473	–772	692	–3,287
(19) Contract labor cost share	–419	3,215	1,947	–1,074	–847	1,795	–101	811
(20) Square feet of building space per acre of land	–4,320	–2,565	46	–1,861	–2,073	–2,210	13,989	637
(21) Square feet of building space per unique patient	8,478	20,689	25,534	–9,730	5,398	–2,558	–4,273	–50,468
(22) Research costs per 1,000 unique patients	30,479	–19,609	688	–20,383	8,209	–24,544	–7,448	–42,644
Sum of Differences—rows (4) through (22)	73,884	13,808	131,429	–94,318	67,291	–27,318	–63,577	–244,692

Table 3.7—continued

	VISN 9	VISN 10	VISN 11	VISN 12	VISN 15	VISN 16	VISN 17	VISN 18
(1) Simulated allocations from SVM with VERA-10	960,519	743,647	850,192	990,930	719,407	1,708,003	929,633	794,982
(2) Unadjusted average allocation	987,411	722,443	850,068	838,993	771,419	1,841,652	961,778	902,576
(3) Difference (1)–(2)	–26,891	21,205	125	151,937	–52,012	–133,649	–32,145	–107,594
Patient characteristics								
(4) Age	972	–1,477	–1,002	–2,332	1,893	5,158	–1,022	1,448
(5) Gender	–773	–503	–638	–573	–784	–284	1,380	765
(6) Physicians per capita	–7,202	–1,302	–1,358	3,908	–7,204	–3,985	–1,172	911
(7) Hospital beds per capita	2,338	–2,672	–2,294	–2,282	3,684	5,845	–522	–2,178
(8) Rural or urban status	–6,104	1,648	–439	842	–5,850	–4,886	884	–642
(9) Distance to closest facility	745	–4,011	270	–2,654	348	5,226	3,696	4,160
(10) Distance to closest CBOC	3,690	–8,324	2,556	–7,433	181	36,376	–2,811	9,211
(11) Medicare reliance	19,835	–11,340	–390	17,826	14,854	–7,298	–9,783	19,633
(12) Medicaid generosity for LTC	152	4,084	902	1,299	512	–4,857	–2,465	–3,470
(13) VERA-10 health status measure	–29,745	54,147	–956	96,994	–22,825	–119,815	–8,942	–61,458
Facility characteristics								
(14) Rural or urban status	4,512	–1,617	–7,893	–3,129	–6,520	1,384	4,403	328
(15) Residents per full-time MD	6,326	–2,201	–3,725	5,848	11,076	–4,625	861	–2,570
(16) VA labor index	–15,623	1,559	1,685	15,542	–12,209	–19,066	–21,198	–23,073
(17) Average food cost per bed day	5,326	–3,014	2,696	688	3,999	–3,113	–5,033	–5,969
(18) Energy price ($/million Btus)	750	175	940	336	37	4,249	2,791	–820
(19) Contract labor cost share	1,373	–1,204	–74	1,066	–872	–933	1,431	–578
(20) Square feet of building space per acre of land	–3,311	–1,321	3,178	4,650	–3,733	17,536	–3,749	–3,656
(21) Square feet of building space per unique patient	4,306	4,622	8,139	19,996	–1,104	–16,448	2,257	–23,654
(22) Research costs per 1,000 unique patients	–14,458	–6,045	–1,470	1,343	–27,493	–24,113	6,849	–15,980
Sum of Differences—rows (4) through (22)	–26,891	21,205	125	151,936	–52,012	–133,649	–32,145	–107,593

Table 3.7—continued

	VISN 19	VISN 20	VISN 21	VISN 22	VISN 23
(1) Simulated allocations from SVM with VERA-10	526,247	933,693	1,093,188	1,204,542	979,479
(2) Unadjusted average allocation	557,628	900,785	932,915	1,103,463	919,837
(3) Difference (1)–(2)	–31,381	32,908	160,273	101,079	59,642
Patient characteristics					
(4) Age	–515	–1,169	3,306	–510	–1,149
(5) Gender	632	1,629	585	515	–707
(6) Physicians per capita	–653	–3,372	4,193	6,621	–6,780
(7) Hospital beds per capita	–476	–3,785	–3,551	–5,301	3,975
(8) Rural or urban status	–3,457	–1,856	3,200	8,493	–7,921
(9) Distance to closest facility	5,263	–361	3,731	–1,629	9,347
(10) Distance to closest CBOC	554	6,199	–515	–15,339	12,649
(11) Medicare reliance	9,621	10,328	5,503	–37,046	35,630
(12) Medicaid generosity for LTC	880	469	–1,451	–2,329	2,713
(13) VERA-10 health status measure	–24,845	5,176	5,051	18,291	8,213
Facility characteristics					
(14) Rural or urban status	–7,493	–3,977	4,061	4,864	32
(15) Residents per full-time MD	–321	–9,006	–2,973	11,752	16,098
(16) VA labor index	–2,792	4,347	68,519	27,436	–4,739
(17) Average food cost per bed day	747	2,834	8,056	12,816	–4,895
(18) Energy price ($/million Btus)	641	1,195	–1,224	–1,094	921
(19) Contract labor cost share	–1,575	–255	–2,437	–2,179	910
(20) Square feet of building space per acre of land	–637	–4,899	231	–983	–4,949
(21) Square feet of building space per unique patient	–3,158	2,905	–6,571	1,865	13,776
(22) Research costs per 1,000 unique patients	–3,797	26,505	72,557	74,835	–13,481
Sum of Differences—rows (4) through (22)	–31,381	32,908	160,272	101,078	59,641

NOTE: Figures shown are in thousands of dollars.

Table 3.8
Disaggregation of Simulated Allocations from the Selected Variables Model with VA DCGs

	VISN 1	VISN 2	VISN 3	VISN 4	VISN 5	VISN 6	VISN 7	VISN 8
(1) Simulated allocations from SVM with VA DCGs	993,664	582,579	1,058,272	969,658	596,833	964,141	1,162,743	1,640,071
(2) Unadjusted average allocation	947,153	567,019	917,287	1,131,336	544,274	1,021,624	1,231,463	1,874,403
(3) Difference (1)–(2)	46,511	15,561	140,984	−161,679	52,559	−57,483	−68,720	−234,331
Patient characteristics								
(4) Age	−4,329	−3,617	−6,852	−5,714	−325	2,956	4,774	−4,288
(5) Gender	−786	−318	−1,838	−1,543	765	1,389	1,556	−427
(6) Physicians per capita	3,201	−477	6,110	381	1,783	−3,655	−2,817	1,720
(7) Hospital beds per capita	−1,438	618	1,018	2,072	1,214	−360	829	2,686
(8) Rural or urban status	886	526	5,124	1,707	1,738	−1,381	−1,252	6,794
(9) Distance to closest facility	−6,308	4,389	−10,914	−9,541	−5,340	−2,916	1,262	102
(10) Distance to closest CBOC	−3,911	−3,082	−6,593	−4,638	−3,306	7,773	4,866	−6,610
(11) Medicare reliance	2,892	5,870	−12,403	−21,965	−26	1,214	−6,989	−15,168
(12) Medicaid generosity for LTC	10,247	5,759	7,005	8,159	−1,834	−5,562	−6,087	−8,242
(13) VA DCG health status measure	−5,667	12,215	79,177	−94,584	25,592	−13,755	−54,346	−71,111
Facility characteristics								
(14) Rural or urban status	−6,751	2,083	3,035	−380	1,947	735	−364	7,014
(15) Residents per full-time MD	38	263	−137	1,904	31	2,066	−350	5,064
(16) VA labor index	18,398	−7,130	47,267	−2,973	14,225	−15,076	−17,560	−60,997
(17) Average food cost per bed day	80	−1,872	−1,092	−218	−89	−432	−297	−107
(18) Energy price ($/million Btus)	5,673	3,068	3,440	73	4,451	2,333	−2,090	9,931
(19) Contract labor cost share	247	−1,892	−1,146	632	498	−1,056	59	−477
(20) Square feet of building space per acre of land	−6,983	−4,146	74	−3,007	−3,351	−3,572	22,611	1,029
(21) Square feet of building space per unique patient	9,629	23,499	29,002	−11,051	6,131	−2,905	−4,853	−57,322
(22) Research costs per 1,000 unique patients	31,391	−20,196	708	−20,992	8,455	−25,278	−7,671	−43,920
Sum of Differences—rows (4) through (22)	46,510	15,560	140,984	−161,678	52,558	−57,483	−68,720	−234,330

Table 3.8—continued

	VISN 9	VISN 10	VISN 11	VISN 12	VISN 15	VISN 16	VISN 17	VISN 18
(1) Simulated allocations from SVM with VA DCGs	976,477	751,565	835,871	1,004,644	748,813	1,676,286	901,935	813,545
(2) Unadjusted average allocation	987,411	722,443	850,068	838,993	771,419	1,841,652	961,778	902,576
(3) Difference (1)–(2)	–10,934	29,122	–14,197	165,651	–22,606	–165,366	–59,843	–89,030
Patient characteristics								
(4) Age	2,518	–738	–782	–3,425	197	6,893	2,828	1,017
(5) Gender	–748	–487	–618	–555	–759	–275	1,336	740
(6) Physicians per capita	–3,845	–1,182	–300	269	–2,640	–2,027	–299	383
(7) Hospital beds per capita	1,673	–1,500	–1,161	–484	2,214	4,063	–392	–2,301
(8) Rural or urban status	–5,407	1,470	–242	599	–5,177	–3,972	754	–360
(9) Distance to closest facility	903	–4,864	328	–3,218	422	6,338	4,483	5,045
(10) Distance to closest CBOC	1,546	–3,488	1,071	–3,115	76	15,242	–1,178	3,860
(11) Medicare reliance	9,438	–6,347	–2,542	9,651	6,461	–4,204	–2,705	13,231
(12) Medicaid generosity for LTC	404	10,834	2,392	3,447	1,357	–12,883	–6,540	–9,204
(13) VA DCG health status measure	16,312	36,752	–18,240	118,101	32,664	–125,589	–29,589	–30,117
Facility characteristics								
(14) Rural or urban status	3,667	–156	–8,109	–1,987	–5,298	86	3,593	2,801
(15) Residents per full-time MD	–2,116	736	1,246	–1,956	–3,706	1,547	–288	860
(16) VA labor index	–18,270	1,823	1,971	18,175	–14,278	–22,296	–24,789	–26,982
(17) Average food cost per bed day	1,417	–802	717	183	1,064	–828	–1,339	–1,588
(18) Energy price ($/million Btus)	–2,267	–527	–2,839	–1,016	–112	–12,839	–8,434	2,479
(19) Contract labor cost share	–808	708	44	–628	513	549	–842	340
(20) Square feet of building space per acre of land	–5,351	–2,135	5,137	7,515	–6,033	28,344	–6,059	–5,909
(21) Square feet of building space per unique patient	4,890	5,250	9,244	22,712	–1,254	–18,682	2,563	–26,866
(22) Research costs per 1,000 unique patients	–14,891	–6,226	–1,514	1,384	–28,316	–24,834	7,054	–16,458
Sum of Differences—rows (4) through (22)	–10,934	29,122	–14,197	165,651	–22,605	–165,366	–59,843	–89,030

Table 3.8—continued

	VISN 19	VISN 20	VISN 21	VISN 22	VISN 23
(1) Simulated allocations from SVM with VA DCGs	587,963	975,788	1,103,342	1,174,447	1,006,892
(2) Unadjusted average allocation	557,628	900,785	932,915	1,103,463	919,837
(3) Difference (1)–(2)	30,336	75,003	170,427	70,983	87,054
Patient characteristics					
(4) Age	760	4,395	2,635	5,563	–4,465
(5) Gender	612	1,577	566	498	–684
(6) Physicians per capita	98	–971	2,003	4,971	–2,706
(7) Hospital beds per capita	–862	–3,127	–3,402	–4,338	2,979
(8) Rural or urban status	–3,128	–1,335	2,769	6,733	–6,845
(9) Distance to closest facility	6,383	–438	4,525	–1,975	11,337
(10) Distance to closest CBOC	232	2,598	–216	–6,427	5,300
(11) Medicare reliance	5,677	9,219	6,307	–14,639	17,030
(12) Medicaid generosity for LTC	2,334	1,243	–3,850	–6,176	7,196
(13) VA DCG health status measure	34,877	38,178	–235	–30,919	80,283
Facility characteristics					
(14) Rural or urban status	–4,151	–4,405	3,288	3,939	–587
(15) Residents per full-time MD	107	3,013	995	–3,932	–5,385
(16) VA labor index	–3,265	5,083	80,129	32,085	–5,541
(17) Average food cost per bed day	199	754	2,143	3,409	–1,302
(18) Energy price ($/million Btus)	–1,935	–3,610	3,697	3,304	–2,782
(19) Contract labor cost share	927	150	1,434	1,282	–535
(20) Square feet of building space per acre of land	–1,030	–7,919	373	–1,589	–7,999
(21) Square feet of building space per unique patient	–3,587	3,299	–7,463	2,118	15,646
(22) Research costs per 1,000 unique patients	–3,910	27,298	74,728	77,074	–13,885
Sum of Differences—rows (4) through (22)	30,336	75,002	170,426	70,982	87,054

NOTE: Figures shown are in thousands of dollars.

Table 3.9
Total Amount of Money Redistributed by Each Variable in the Selected Variables Model

Variable	Selected Variables Model with VERA-10			Selected Variables Model with VA DCGs		
	Rank	Total Amount	% of Approp	Rank	Total Amount	% of Approp
Health status measure	1	381,952	1.861%	1	393,868	1.919%
Research costs per 1,000 unique patients	2	221,466	1.079%	2	228,092	1.111%
VA labor index	3	187,405	0.913%	3	219,157	1.068%
Medicare reliance	4	157,255	0.766%	5	69,959	0.341%
Square feet of building space per unique patient	5	117,964	0.575%	4	118,337	0.577%
Distance to closest CBOC	6	101,580	0.495%	9	37,264	0.182%
Residents per full-time MD	7	53,418	0.260%	15	17,870	0.087%
Physicians per capita	8	49,094	0.239%	14	20,918	0.102%
Square feet of building space per acre of land	9	40,267	0.196%	6	65,083	0.317%
Rural or urban status—facility	10	39,299	0.191%	12	32,188	0.157%
Distance to closest facility	11	37,529	0.183%	11	34,179	0.167%
Average food cost per bed day	12	37,462	0.183%	17	9,967	0.049%
Rural or urban status—patient	13	35,154	0.171%	13	29,099	0.142%
Hospital beds per capita	14	25,729	0.125%	16	16,388	0.080%
Medicaid generosity for LTC	15	22,762	0.111%	7	53,180	0.259%
Age	16	17,009	0.083%	10	34,535	0.168%
Energy price ($/million Btus)	17	12,726	0.062%	8	38,450	0.187%
Contract labor cost share	18	12,547	0.061%	19	7,384	0.036%
Gender	19	9,338	0.045%	18	9,039	0.044%

NOTES: Variables are ranked by total amount redistributed under the SVM with VERA-10. Figures shown are in thousands of dollars.

CHAPTER FOUR

Conclusions and Policy Implications

In Chapter Three, we presented our analyses of the patient and facility characteristics that influence the costs of providing care to veterans under VERA. We first presented the results of several regression equations in which we quantified the independent effects of these characteristics on the annual costs of care. We then simulated how VISN allocations would change, in comparison to actual FY 2003 allocations, if one were to use the regression-based approach and control for a wider range of variables. Finally, in the disaggregation analysis, we examined how each variable included in our models affects VISN-level allocations.

Our regression results were very consistent with those published in the Phase II report, which relied on patient-level data from 2000 rather than 2001. Some of the key regression findings are as follows:

- The proportion of VA patient care costs explained by each of the regression equations ranged from a low of 0.46 for the BRM to a high of 0.62 in the VA DCGs SVM.
- The case-mix variables (i.e., VERA-10 and VA DCGs) included in the regression equations were highly significant and behaved as expected, with higher resource use being associated with patients in higher case-mix categories.
- As expected, age and gender independently affect patient care costs, controlling for alternative case-mix measures and other factors.
- As expected, patients treated at VA facilities who are more reliant on Medicare providers incur lower VA costs than do those patients who receive little or no care from Medicare providers.
- Contrary to our expectations, costs are higher for those veterans who must travel longer distances for care.
- We found that many facility-level characteristics had significant positive effects on patient health care costs across both case-mix specifications, including the VISN labor index, research costs per patient, food costs per bed day, and square feet of building space, both per patient and per acre of land.
- In contrast, for three variables in the SVM, the direction of the association with costs depends on which health status measure is included in the model. For example, when the VERA-10 measure was used, the number of residents per full-time physician had a positive effect on patient costs, but it had a negative effect when VA DCGs served as the case-mix measure. Similarly, energy prices and contract labor costs were negatively associated with costs when VERA-10 was the case-mix measure, but were positively associated with costs under VA DCGs.

There were, however, some differences between these results and the results of the Phase II analysis. In particular, recent VERA policy changes—including the introduction of the VERA-10 case-mix adjustment and the manner in which high-cost cases (i.e., those with costs of $70,000 or more) are treated under VERA—have reduced differences in the ways funds are allocated under the current VERA system and the regression-based approach. For example, in FY 2002, applying the regression-based approach—in particular, the VERA-10 SVM—would have redistributed 2.9 percent of the total actual allocation. However, in FY 2003, the regression-based approach with VERA-10 would have redistributed only 1.2 percent of the funds. VA DCGs would lead to a slightly larger redistribution (i.e., 1.8 percent of the total allocation).

One of the major contributions of this study was to "disaggregate" the results, so that the unique impact of each explanatory variable on simulated allocations could be identified. The results of this analysis revealed that case mix, research costs, the labor index, Medicare reliance, and the number of square feet of building space per patient result in the largest redistributions of funds. In contrast, contract labor cost share and gender had very little impact on how funds are allocated. This finding suggests that if the VA considers adding more variables to the VERA allocation formula, case mix, research costs, the labor index, Medicare reliance, and the number of square feet of building space per patient ought to have higher priorities than other factors.

A key finding and conclusion from both the results presented in this report and the Phase II analysis is that case mix is crucial in explaining differences in patients' costs and that it varies across VISNs. In our earlier report (Wasserman et al., 2003), we recommended that the VA adopt a more-refined case-mix adjustment methodology—either VERA-10 or VA DCGs—than the one it had used since VERA's inception, which relied on only three categories. Subsequently, the VA adopted the VERA-10 case-mix measure. We applaud this decision, as we believe that it will lead to a more efficient and equitable division of health care resources.

What is less clear, however, is whether VERA could be further improved by moving from VERA-10 to VA DCGs. On the one hand, the R-squared values in our regression equations demonstrate that VA DCGs better explain patient-level cost variation than does VERA-10. On the other hand, we observed that the VA DCGs would shift a substantial amount of money across VISNs, and we know little about why such redistributions would occur. Although they could be the result of actual case-mix differences that the VERA-10 case-mix measure fails to take into account, it is also possible that some VISNs do better than others under VA DCGs simply because they have captured patients' diagnosis and procedure codes more completely. In addition, a patient could be assigned to a high-cost VA DCG on the basis of a single diagnosis code, even if that diagnosis code is not the principal one and even if the patient relies mainly on Medicare rather than on the VA for his or her care. Thus, it is possible that VA DCGs would be more susceptible to gaming than is VERA-10. In light of such concerns, we believe that additional analytic work should be undertaken before the VA introduces VA DCGs. Such analytic work should focus on clarifying why funds shift across VISNs in moving from VERA-10 to VA DCGs, as well as determining how well VA DCGs do in explaining costs for certain clinical subpopulations (including the chronically mentally ill and patients requiring long-term care services), and evaluating whether VA DCGs are more susceptible to gaming than is VERA-10.

As we found in the Phase II analysis, Medicare reliance continues to have a statistically significant effect on the costs of treating veterans at VA facilities. Specifically, as one might expect, the greater the degree to which individuals rely on Medicare, the lower their VA costs. Consequently, we believe that the VA should consider modifying VISN allocations to adjust for differences in the degree to which VA patients rely on Medicare providers for the care they receive. Doing so would help make the VERA system more equitable and efficient. However, prior to implementing a Medicare reliance adjustment, we believe that the VA should investigate the accuracy with which Medicare data, which necessarily lag the VA data by a year and which contain no cost information on HMO patients, predict future Medicare expenditures.

Study Limitations

Many of the study limitations noted in the Phase II analysis apply here as well. First, although the analysis generated insight into factors that explain variation in patients' costs, we are unable to compare, for example, the average cost per patient and any sort of efficiency "gold standard." In other words, we have no way of knowing what the "right" costs should be for any given patient. Rather, we are able to compare only how costs vary for patients with different patient, facility, and community characteristics. This problem is exacerbated by the fact that the necessary data are not available to adjust our cost data for differences in quality of care across facilities and VISNs.

Second, the validity of our analysis ultimately depends to a great extent on the completeness and quality of the data that were used to construct the patient and facility equations. In general, we found the patient-level data to be quite complete, with the exception of certain variables such as income. Although we did not attempt to validate a sample of the patient data against data drawn from patients' medical records, we did conduct a variety of reliability and validation checks using data from multiple years on the same set of patients. From what we could determine, the patient-level data appeared to be of very high quality. However, we continue to maintain that the quality and completeness of the facility data could be improved. To some extent, the problems that we encountered in the facility data set were due to the large number of management consolidations that occurred over the last half dozen years or so. Often, we ran into difficulty obtaining data on all measures for the same set of facilities. We believe that if the VA chooses to adopt an allocation methodology that accounts for facility-level characteristics, such as our regression/simulation approach, the quality of the facility data collection process should be improved. Specifically, the definition of what constitutes a facility should be developed (e.g., a management unit or physical location) and applied consistently throughout the data collection process.

Value of the Regression-Based Approach

In both this and the Phase II report, we used regression analysis to understand the extent to which a wide range of variables influences the costs of caring for VA patients. This allowed us to examine each of the factors of interest to the Congress, as expressed in the legislation that mandated our VERA analyses, as well as a host of other factors identified through the relevant literature and our Phase I interviews that could influence patient care costs. We found that regression techniques provided a powerful tool for (1) identifying those factors that influence costs, (2) predicting patients' costs after controlling for a wide range of variables, and (3) providing the inputs for the subsequent simulation and disaggregation analyses.

We believe that regression analysis holds great potential for serving as a mechanism for the VA to determine VISN-level allocations. However, we do not believe that it is critical at this juncture to shift to a regression-based allocation approach. The primary reason we advocate against such a transition at this point is that such a change would be difficult to implement, and, as we indicated earlier, the current allocation approach comes very close to the regression-based one, as evidenced by the low percentage of funds that the latter would redistribute. In the event that the VA elects to adjust VISN allocations for a wider range of variables—including, for example, Medicare reliance and some of the other factors that the disaggregation analysis demonstrated were responsible for shifting funds across VISNs—then adopting a regression-based approach might prove to be advantageous.

Even if the VA does not switch to a regression-based methodology, the use of regression analysis can provide a powerful management tool for VA headquarters staff and VISN directors. The single-equation approach upon which this study relied is easy to use and interpret. The output from the regression models—both the SVM and AVM—can be used to identify additional potential adjustments to VERA, inform decisions regarding requests for supplemental funds, and provide guidance for VISN directors in determining how funds should be allocated to facilities within their networks.

Key Formulas and Data in the FY 2003 VERA

In FY 2003, VERA allocated nearly $24 billion to cover the costs of patient care. Of this $24 billion, $5.1 billion was available for care of patients in the four Complex Care groups, $12.5 billion was available for patients in the six Basic Care Groups, and nearly $1.4 billion was allocated to those VISNs with patients whose care costs were in the top 1 percent (those whose costs exceed $70,000).

In addition, nearly $1.6 billion was allocated to support research, education, equipment purchases, and NRM expenses. The allocation for research is $400 million, based on the estimates for medical care support to research as submitted in the president's FY 2003 medical programs budget request. Education support continues to be allocated on the basis of the number of medical residents in a VISN. Equipment and NRM funds continue to be allocated on the basis of workload. NRM is adjusted for geographic differences in construction costs. Table A.1 explains the formulas used to allocate VERA funds in FY 2003.

Table A.1
Key Formulas and Data in the FY 2003 VERA

Allocation Factors	Total Dollars Allocated	Mechanism to Determine Total Dollars	Definitions of Workload (Unit of Measure)	National Total Workload (Unit of Measure)	National Price/Allocation Rate
Basic Care (Sum of 6 Basic Care Price Groups)	$12,478,652,268	67.2% of Basic Care and Complex Care dollars available. The Basic Care and Complex Care dollars are the total General Purpose (GP) funding less the funding for Research Support, Education Support, Equipment and Non-Recurring Maintenance (NRM). The percentage for each group is updated based on FY 2001 DSS cost experience.	Number of patients in the 3-year "Cat A/X" user file. Three-year file includes FYs 1999, 2000, and 2001 patients who rely on VA for their care. There are 6 Basic Care Price Groups, and each includes VERA Patient Classes described below. Workload units based on historical utilization are adjusted to reflect care provided in more than one network.	3,779,887	Each of the 6 Basic Care Price Groups has a separate price based on the dollars allocated divided by the total workload
1. Non-Reliant Care	$116,547,124	0.62% of Basic Care and Complex Care dollars, less the High Cost Payments of $923,491.	This group includes 4 Patient Classes: 1) Employee/ Collaterals; 2) Pharmacy; 3) Compensation and Pension Exams; and 4) Non-Vested Patients. The FY 2001 patient workload in the Employee/Collaterals and Pharmacy classes is only included under the VERA methodology in conjunction with care delivered to that veteran in other classes.	443,477	$263 per Non-Reliant Care Basic Care Workload Unit
2. Basic Medical	$4,169,216,455	22.20% of Basic Care and Complex Care dollars, less the High Cost Payments of $35,298,984.	This group includes 5 Patient Classes: 5) Ear, Nose, and Throat; 6) Other Acute Diseases; 7) Endocrine, Nutritional, and Metabolic Disorders; 8) Central Nervous System, and 9) Musculoskeletal Disorders.	1,727,650	$2,413 per Basic Medical Basic Care Workload Unit
3. Mental Health	$1,076,150,278	5.71% of Basic Care and Complex Care dollars, less the High Cost Payments of $4,988,266.	This group includes 2 Patient Classes: 10) Acute Mental Disease and 11) Addictive Disorders.	302,092	$3,562 per Mental Health Basic Care Workload Unit
4. Heart/Lung/GI	$2,910,016,343	15.69% of Basic Care and Complex Care dollars, less the High Cost Payments of $61,573,577.	This group includes 3 Patient Classes: 12) Cardiovascular Disease, 13) Gastroenterology Disorder, and 14) Pulmonary Disease.	781,904	$3,722 per Heart/Lung/GI Basic Care Workload Unit
5. Oncology	$889,650,052	4.87% of Basic Care and Complex Care dollars, less the High Cost Payments of $32,159,501.	This group includes 3 Patient Classes: 15) Hepatitis C without Anti-viral Therapy; 16) HIV without Anti-retroviral Therapy; and 17) Oncology.	106,711	$8,337 per Oncology/Infectious Disease Basic Care Workload Unit
6. Multiple Problem	$3,317,072,016	18.14% of Basic Care and Complex Care dollars, less the High Cost Payments of $117,579,579.	This group includes 4 Patient Classes: 18) Medical Psychiatric + Substance Abuse; 19) Psychiatric + Substance Abuse; 20) Multiple Medical; and 21) Posttraumatic Stress Disorder (PTSD) Acute.	418,053	$7,935 per Multiple Medical Basic Care Workload Unit
Subtotal	$12,478,652,268				

Table A.1—continued

Allocation Factors	Total Dollars Allocated	Mechanism to Determine Total Dollars	Definitions of Workload (Unit of Measure)	National Total Workload (Unit of Measure)	National Price/Allocation Rate
Complex Care (Sum of 4 Complex Care Price Groups)	$5,063,193,869	32.8% of Basic Care and Complex Care dollars available. The Basic and Complex Care dollars are the total GP funding less the funding for Research Support, Education Support, Equipment, and NRM. The percentage for each group is updated based on FY 2001 cost experience.	Number of Complex Care patients forecasted to use the VISN in FY 2003. This one-year forecasted number is based on historical utilization over five years (FYs 1997–2001). Workload units based on historical utilization are adjusted to reflect care provided in more than one network. The forecast continues to include a factor for age, but no longer for veteran population trends.	155,739	Each of the 4 Complex Care Price Groups has a separate price based on the dollars allocated divided by the total workload
7. Specialized Care	$926,779,306	5.31% of Basic Care and Complex Care dollars, less the High Cost Payments of $79,204,283.	This group includes 5 Patient Classes: 22) Hepatitis C with Anti-viral Therapy; 23) HIV+ with Anti-retroviral Therapy; 24) PTSD Chronic; 25) Home Based Primary Care; and 26) Traumatic Brain Injury.	49,425	$18,751 per Specialized Care Complex Care Workload Unit
8. Supportive Care	$1,703,614,118	10.63% of Basic Care and Complex Care dollars, less the High Cost Payments of $309,408,035.	This group includes 7 Patient Classes: 27) Stroke; 28) Domiciliary; 29) Spinal Cord Injury (SCI) Paraplegic—Old Injury; 30) SCI Quadriplegic—Old Injury; 31) Blind Rehabilitation; 32) Community Nursing Home; and 33) LTC: Low Activities of Daily Living.	57,207	$29,780 per Supportive Care Complex Care Workload Unit
9. Chronic Mental Illness	$1,037,311,095	6.55% of Basic Care and Complex Care dollars, less the High Cost Payments of $202,527,713.	This group includes 4 Patient Classes: 34) Mental Health Intensive Case Management; 35) Other Psychosis; 36) Substance Abuse; and 37) Schizophrenia and Dementia.	26,296	$39,448 per Chronic Mental Illness Complex Care Workload Unit
10. Critically Ill	$1,395,489,350	10.28% of Basic Care and Complex Care dollars, less the High Cost Payments of $551,471,434.	This group includes 10 Patient Classes: 38) End Stage Renal Disease; 39) SCI Paraplegic—New Injury; 40) SCI Quadriplegic—New Injury; 41) LTC: Clinical Complex; 42) LTC: Behavioral; 43) LTC: Physical; 44) LTC: Rehabilitation; 45) LTC: Specialized Care; 46) Transplants; and 47) Ventilator Dependent.	22,811	$61,177 per Critically Ill Complex Care Workload Unit
Subtotal	$5,063,193,869				

Table A.1—continued

Allocation Factors	Total Dollars Allocated	Mechanism to Determine Total Dollars	Definitions of Workload (Unit of Measure)	National Total Workload (Unit of Measure)	National Price/Allocation Rate
High Cost Patient Funding	$1,395,134,863	Patient costs that exceed $70,000 (1% of High-Cost Patients) are removed from the pool of funds for each of the 10 Price Groups.	Networks receive an additional allocation equal to the amount that these costs exceeded the $70,000 threshold.	29,928	An average of $40,815 for Basic Care Patients and $48,128 for Complex Care Patients nationally
Geographic Price Adjustment	$0	The Geographic Price Adjustment (labor index) is applied against $14.05 billion labor, contractual labor and Non-labor contractual goods dollars expended in FY 2001, which is approximately 66% of FY 2001 total obligations.	The FY 2003 VERA labor index is computed using 4 pay periods of FY 2001 normal pay data only and a national market basket methodology. The adjustment continues (as began in FY 2002) to account for local cost of living factors associated with procuring contracted labor and Non-labor contractual goods, such as energy related products, utilities, and provisions. For FY 2003, the labor index methodology for computing is unchanged.		
Research support	$400,375,000	Total of research support funds in the FY 2003 President's budget.	Dollars of FY 2001 funded research (intra- and extra-mural research). Applies weights: 100% for VA administered research; 75% for peer reviewed research that is not VA administered; 25% for non-peer reviewed research that is not VA administered.	$881,818,194 unweighted; $740,057,493 weighted	$0.54 per dollar of Reported Research
Education support	$355,599,000	Total of education support funds in the FY 2003 President's budget.	Number of residents for Academic Year 2002/2003.	8,787	$40,469 per Resident
Subtotal	$2,151,108,863				

Table A.1—continued

Allocation Factors	Total Dollars Allocated	Mechanism to Determine Total Dollars	Definitions of Workload (Unit of Measure)	National Total Workload (Unit of Measure)	National Price/Allocation Rate
Equipment—capitation	$577,708,000	Total of equipment funds in the FY 2003 President's budget.	The Equipment allocation is based totally on prorated patient (PRP) workload (Sum of Basic Care (6 price groups) and Complex Care (4 price groups) workload).	3,935,626	$147
NRM—Boeckh Index times total workload NEW MODEL	$254,865,000	Derived from NRM funds in the FY 2003 President's budget.	The NRM allocation is based on workload adjusted by the Boeckh Index (Workload (PRPs) times Boeckh Index). This Boeckh Index is an external inflation index that measures the relative cost of building and/or renovating space.	74,365	$3,427
Total Capital Accounts	$832,573,000	Derived from the FY 2003 President's budget.			
VERA Capping	$0	Network allocations are adjusted to assure all have a gain over FY 2002 of at least 5%. Allocations for networks with largest gains from FY 2002 are adjusted to a maximum of 12.6% to fund the increases of networks up to the 5% level.	Networks receiving an increased or decreased adjustment (dollars in thousands): Network 3 (+$38,171); Network 4 (–$6,352); Network 8 (–$32,580); Network 16 (–$510); Network 22 (–$12,170); Network 23 (+$13,440).		
Total $ General Purpose	$20,525,528,000	Derived from FY 2003 Medical Care budget less Specific Purpose funding.			

SOURCE: Adapted from the VERA Book (2003).

VISN-Level Patient Variables and Descriptive Statistics for the FY 2001 VHA Patient Population

Tables B.1 and B.2 describe the characteristics of the VHA patient population and facilities by VISN for fiscal year 2001. Table B.1 shows the size, demographic characteristics, and other patient-level variables for the patient population. Table B.2 describes the facility-level characteristics. Table 2.1 in Chapter Two shows the variable included in the SVM.

Table B.1
VISN-Level Descriptors: Patient Variables

VISN	Number of Individuals	Age							
		Under 25	25 to 34	35 to 44	45 to 54	55 to 64	65 to 74	75 to 84	85 or older
01 Boston	194,474	0.010	0.036	0.072	0.182	0.158	0.270	0.247	0.026
02 Albany	122,490	0.024	0.049	0.092	0.182	0.154	0.244	0.229	0.027
03 Bronx	193,469	0.015	0.038	0.072	0.156	0.146	0.273	0.269	0.031
04 Pittsburgh	239,004	0.010	0.032	0.068	0.169	0.154	0.289	0.257	0.022
05 Baltimore	100,650	0.009	0.048	0.117	0.225	0.158	0.228	0.193	0.021
06 Durham	196,907	0.012	0.056	0.111	0.237	0.176	0.225	0.169	0.015
07 Atlanta	238,002	0.012	0.050	0.114	0.239	0.177	0.226	0.167	0.015
08 Bay Pines	392,003	0.009	0.035	0.079	0.174	0.171	0.267	0.238	0.026
09 Nashville	200,109	0.023	0.054	0.100	0.227	0.179	0.226	0.175	0.017
10 Cincinnati	137,230	0.008	0.043	0.102	0.218	0.159	0.239	0.214	0.018
11 Ann Arbor	173,239	0.012	0.041	0.089	0.207	0.161	0.252	0.221	0.018
12 Chicago	170,090	0.015	0.045	0.087	0.185	0.156	0.256	0.232	0.024
15 Kansas City	159,372	0.008	0.031	0.078	0.200	0.168	0.271	0.223	0.021
16 Jackson	349,952	0.010	0.045	0.090	0.231	0.190	0.235	0.181	0.018
17 Dallas	183,516	0.014	0.057	0.104	0.235	0.189	0.213	0.168	0.019
18 Phoenix	197,510	0.034	0.054	0.094	0.203	0.182	0.227	0.185	0.020
19 Denver	112,454	0.013	0.050	0.091	0.219	0.182	0.231	0.196	0.019
20 Portland	166,760	0.014	0.057	0.109	0.248	0.191	0.196	0.166	0.019
21 San Francisco	181,234	0.020	0.049	0.091	0.230	0.196	0.202	0.187	0.024
22 Long Beach	208,578	0.022	0.064	0.111	0.231	0.200	0.194	0.158	0.019
23 Lincoln & Minneapolis	212,720	0.014	0.036	0.071	0.173	0.150	0.289	0.242	0.025

Table B.1—continued

VISN	Income (in thousands)						Race/Ethnicity				
	Missing	$20 or less	$21 to $40	$41 to $60	$61 to $80	Greater than $80	Hispanic	Native American	Black	Asian	White
01 Boston	0.256	0.405	0.220	0.050	0.021	0.048	0.017	0.002	0.048	0.002	0.931
02 Albany	0.305	0.378	0.203	0.051	0.021	0.042	0.008	0.002	0.072	0.001	0.917
03 Bronx	0.335	0.342	0.180	0.045	0.021	0.078	0.067	0.001	0.214	0.004	0.715
04 Pittsburgh	0.254	0.395	0.220	0.053	0.023	0.055	0.008	0.001	0.142	0.002	0.848
05 Baltimore	0.236	0.440	0.207	0.051	0.024	0.042	0.014	0.001	0.400	0.002	0.582
06 Durham	0.192	0.458	0.236	0.057	0.023	0.035	0.008	0.003	0.278	0.002	0.709
07 Atlanta	0.225	0.470	0.207	0.048	0.019	0.030	0.007	0.001	0.349	0.002	0.642
08 Bay Pines	0.224	0.455	0.206	0.047	0.020	0.049	0.187	0.001	0.098	0.001	0.713
09 Nashville	0.250	0.467	0.198	0.042	0.016	0.028	0.004	0.001	0.147	0.001	0.847
10 Cincinnati	0.183	0.485	0.222	0.049	0.020	0.041	0.007	0.001	0.186	0.001	0.805
11 Ann Arbor	0.277	0.439	0.182	0.043	0.019	0.041	0.007	0.001	0.168	0.004	0.823
12 Chicago	0.271	0.413	0.189	0.051	0.023	0.054	0.015	0.002	0.217	0.004	0.762
15 Kansas City	0.225	0.453	0.206	0.051	0.020	0.045	0.008	0.002	0.115	0.001	0.874
16 Jackson	0.189	0.499	0.219	0.044	0.017	0.031	0.016	0.005	0.238	0.001	0.740
17 Dallas	0.214	0.488	0.210	0.043	0.018	0.027	0.136	0.001	0.150	0.002	0.711
18 Phoenix	0.280	0.419	0.202	0.045	0.019	0.035	0.152	0.020	0.050	0.004	0.774
19 Denver	0.229	0.426	0.218	0.054	0.022	0.050	0.061	0.006	0.043	0.003	0.887
20 Portland	0.204	0.499	0.210	0.040	0.017	0.030	0.017	0.010	0.069	0.015	0.890
21 San Francisco	0.269	0.428	0.205	0.041	0.019	0.039	0.053	0.004	0.114	0.100	0.729
22 Long Beach	0.278	0.466	0.171	0.036	0.016	0.034	0.091	0.005	0.176	0.023	0.706
23 Lincoln & Minneapolis	0.321	0.388	0.172	0.045	0.020	0.055	0.005	0.010	0.036	0.001	0.948

Table B.1—continued

VISN	Gender		Marital Status		# of MDs Per Capita				# of Beds Per Capita		
	Female	Male	Single	Married	Less than 0.001	0.001 to 0.002	0.0021 to 0.003	Greater than 0.003	Less than 0.003	0.003 to 0.006	Greater than 0.006
01 Boston	0.073	0.927	0.403	0.597	0.031	0.251	0.250	0.468	0.431	0.536	0.032
02 Albany	0.087	0.913	0.388	0.612	0.193	0.321	0.094	0.393	0.223	0.706	0.071
03 Bronx	0.068	0.932	0.434	0.566	0.006	0.096	0.441	0.457	0.201	0.728	0.071
04 Pittsburgh	0.061	0.939	0.365	0.635	0.166	0.327	0.239	0.268	0.311	0.553	0.136
05 Baltimore	0.094	0.906	0.480	0.520	0.150	0.205	0.359	0.286	0.631	0.093	0.276
06 Durham	0.095	0.905	0.360	0.640	0.380	0.303	0.154	0.163	0.480	0.389	0.131
07 Atlanta	0.097	0.903	0.372	0.628	0.374	0.232	0.172	0.222	0.441	0.411	0.148
08 Bay Pines	0.081	0.919	0.343	0.657	0.177	0.282	0.346	0.196	0.263	0.625	0.112
09 Nashville	0.097	0.903	0.357	0.643	0.437	0.219	0.026	0.318	0.365	0.489	0.147
10 Cincinnati	0.074	0.926	0.443	0.557	0.289	0.265	0.091	0.355	0.420	0.570	0.010
11 Ann Arbor	0.078	0.922	0.419	0.581	0.337	0.204	0.253	0.207	0.394	0.570	0.036
12 Chicago	0.085	0.915	0.434	0.566	0.225	0.197	0.086	0.493	0.252	0.730	0.018
15 Kansas City	0.062	0.938	0.363	0.637	0.478	0.207	0.184	0.131	0.372	0.407	0.221
16 Jackson	0.079	0.921	0.371	0.629	0.350	0.183	0.189	0.279	0.340	0.480	0.180
17 Dallas	0.109	0.891	0.366	0.634	0.363	0.152	0.262	0.223	0.433	0.480	0.087
18 Phoenix	0.138	0.863	0.367	0.633	0.205	0.251	0.238	0.307	0.577	0.357	0.066
19 Denver	0.091	0.910	0.378	0.622	0.215	0.306	0.333	0.146	0.595	0.306	0.099
20 Portland	0.107	0.894	0.426	0.574	0.182	0.409	0.252	0.156	0.623	0.361	0.016
21 San Francisco	0.118	0.882	0.462	0.538	0.104	0.288	0.355	0.253	0.707	0.267	0.026
22 Long Beach	0.098	0.902	0.540	0.460	0.021	0.360	0.614	0.005	0.635	0.364	0.002
23 Lincoln & Minneapolis	0.077	0.924	0.333	0.667	0.456	0.193	0.157	0.195	0.271	0.530	0.199

Table B.1—continued

VISN	Urbanicity of Residence				Distance to Parent Facility	Distance to Closest CBOC	Priority Status						
	Urban	Suburban	Rural	Very Rural			1	2	3	4	5	6	7
01 Boston	0.760	0.165	0.062	0.013	30.05	13.74	0.200	0.069	0.123	0.040	0.313	0.009	0.247
02 Albany	0.747	0.217	0.026	0.011	63.97	10.87	0.178	0.052	0.104	0.031	0.368	0.011	0.256
03 Bronx	0.983	0.017	0.000	0.000	16.95	5.56	0.160	0.047	0.107	0.026	0.306	0.007	0.347
04 Pittsburgh	0.782	0.159	0.038	0.021	27.17	13.78	0.145	0.058	0.106	0.031	0.378	0.009	0.274
05 Baltimore	0.850	0.097	0.025	0.029	24.02	9.41	0.169	0.067	0.113	0.038	0.421	0.012	0.182
06 Durham	0.665	0.210	0.057	0.068	37.87	39.99	0.222	0.088	0.130	0.041	0.359	0.012	0.148
07 Atlanta	0.661	0.239	0.050	0.051	47.30	31.89	0.193	0.080	0.131	0.048	0.363	0.012	0.175
08 Bay Pines	0.873	0.087	0.019	0.021	45.43	14.68	0.178	0.063	0.120	0.039	0.374	0.008	0.219
09 Nashville	0.574	0.171	0.140	0.114	45.87	25.46	0.220	0.070	0.113	0.045	0.386	0.011	0.155
10 Cincinnati	0.794	0.157	0.041	0.008	30.65	12.46	0.147	0.062	0.113	0.042	0.460	0.009	0.168
11 Ann Arbor	0.701	0.198	0.056	0.044	46.90	25.84	0.151	0.058	0.109	0.037	0.406	0.010	0.229
12 Chicago	0.755	0.138	0.071	0.036	38.82	15.06	0.164	0.051	0.098	0.054	0.381	0.010	0.242
15 Kansas City	0.503	0.196	0.192	0.108	49.10	23.84	0.135	0.058	0.103	0.044	0.419	0.012	0.229
16 Jackson	0.652	0.203	0.098	0.048	52.38	41.46	0.189	0.070	0.113	0.051	0.417	0.009	0.150
17 Dallas	0.758	0.149	0.054	0.039	55.35	20.43	0.232	0.087	0.142	0.040	0.353	0.014	0.132
18 Phoenix	0.714	0.186	0.058	0.042	54.30	35.04	0.272	0.070	0.116	0.028	0.337	0.010	0.166
19 Denver	0.536	0.179	0.197	0.089	71.48	24.51	0.193	0.075	0.123	0.035	0.353	0.012	0.209
20 Portland	0.653	0.238	0.082	0.027	43.68	28.55	0.255	0.093	0.137	0.046	0.332	0.011	0.127
21 San Francisco	0.842	0.131	0.020	0.007	56.52	21.88	0.244	0.073	0.122	0.030	0.362	0.010	0.159
22 Long Beach	0.987	0.008	0.003	0.001	41.78	10.09	0.193	0.067	0.120	0.036	0.420	0.008	0.156
23 Lincoln & Minneapolis	0.459	0.216	0.187	0.138	73.92	35.81	0.167	0.060	0.111	0.036	0.313	0.014	0.299

Table B.1—continued

VISN	Not Eligible	No Reliance	Medicare Reliance								General Medicaid Generosity	Generosity of Medicaid LTC
			FFS—1 to 24%	FFS—25 to 49%	FFS—50 to 74%	FFS—75 to 100%	HMO—1 to 24%	HMO—25 to 49%	HMO—50 to 74%	HMO—75 to 100%		
01 Boston	0.551	0.122	0.080	0.043	0.047	0.075	0.002	0.006	0.014	0.061	7,045	12,873
02 Albany	0.569	0.126	0.087	0.045	0.046	0.068	0.002	0.004	0.014	0.040	8,728	12,377
03 Bronx	0.542	0.105	0.056	0.039	0.054	0.109	0.002	0.005	0.015	0.074	7,638	11,532
04 Pittsburgh	0.546	0.094	0.068	0.041	0.045	0.086	0.002	0.005	0.018	0.096	4,455	10,911
05 Baltimore	0.638	0.134	0.065	0.033	0.036	0.058	0.002	0.003	0.009	0.024	4,165	5,492
06 Durham	0.618	0.118	0.093	0.043	0.043	0.071	0.001	0.001	0.003	0.009	3,347	4,459
07 Atlanta	0.611	0.111	0.085	0.046	0.049	0.082	0.001	0.002	0.003	0.011	2,632	4,738
08 Bay Pines	0.588	0.111	0.060	0.037	0.044	0.079	0.002	0.006	0.017	0.056	2,941	4,945
09 Nashville	0.598	0.128	0.101	0.045	0.044	0.069	0.001	0.001	0.004	0.009	3,362	7,444
10 Cincinnati	0.592	0.107	0.072	0.039	0.040	0.075	0.002	0.005	0.014	0.055	5,016	14,855
11 Ann Arbor	0.575	0.117	0.089	0.051	0.053	0.090	0.001	0.002	0.005	0.019	3,996	8,615
12 Chicago	0.564	0.133	0.086	0.043	0.046	0.083	0.002	0.005	0.009	0.029	4,382	9,465
15 Kansas City	0.543	0.135	0.095	0.049	0.052	0.091	0.001	0.003	0.009	0.021	4,080	8,000
16 Jackson	0.608	0.123	0.083	0.038	0.039	0.069	0.001	0.003	0.009	0.027	2,446	3,791
17 Dallas	0.655	0.116	0.064	0.030	0.031	0.052	0.002	0.005	0.012	0.034	2,036	3,823
18 Phoenix	0.627	0.123	0.067	0.032	0.032	0.058	0.004	0.007	0.016	0.035	1,991	2,301
19 Denver	0.599	0.122	0.095	0.041	0.041	0.066	0.002	0.004	0.009	0.021	3,090	9,199
20 Portland	0.635	0.133	0.075	0.029	0.028	0.042	0.003	0.005	0.014	0.037	2,076	7,806
21 San Francisco	0.647	0.121	0.056	0.028	0.029	0.046	0.003	0.008	0.020	0.044	2,348	5,017
22 Long Beach	0.682	0.099	0.033	0.018	0.021	0.037	0.003	0.008	0.023	0.076	2,251	4,332
23 Lincoln & Minneapolis	0.546	0.116	0.116	0.057	0.057	0.090	0.001	0.002	0.004	0.010	5,985	11,078

Table B.2
VISN-Level Descriptors: Facility-Level Variables

| VISN | Urbanicity of Facility | | | | Residents Per Full-Time MD | VA Labor Index | Average Food Cost Per Bed Day | Energy Price (dollars per million Btus) | Contract Labor Costs (% of total labor costs) | Square Feet of Building Space Per Acre of Land | Square Feet of Building Space Per Unique Patient |
	Urban	Suburban	Rural	Very Rural							
01 Boston	0.770	0.135	0.096	0.000	0.715	102.40	6.59	10.22	5.93	10.79	38.15
02 Albany	1.000	0.000	0.000	0.000	0.688	97.87	3.07	10.00	0.22	10.93	53.73
03 Bronx	1.000	0.000	0.000	0.000	0.705	107.67	5.13	9.69	3.51	18.54	49.64
04 Pittsburgh	0.933	0.067	0.000	0.000	0.589	99.26	6.23	8.74	6.23	16.63	28.50
05 Baltimore	1.000	0.000	0.000	0.000	0.701	103.38	6.24	10.62	6.77	11.88	38.97
06 Durham	0.936	0.064	0.000	0.000	0.579	97.58	6.02	9.23	3.82	15.53	31.62
07 Atlanta	0.920	0.080	0.000	0.000	0.735	97.65	6.19	8.31	5.51	43.16	31.20
08 Bay Pines	0.999	0.001	0.000	0.000	0.509	95.20	6.32	10.00	4.84	20.36	18.13
09 Nashville	0.999	0.001	0.001	0.000	0.882	97.13	7.63	8.16	4.14	13.56	34.66
10 Cincinnati	0.895	0.001	0.104	0.000	0.646	99.99	5.30	8.54	6.94	16.44	36.82
11 Ann Arbor	0.716	0.284	0.000	0.000	0.600	99.96	7.30	7.90	5.51	26.72	39.15
12 Chicago	0.835	0.090	0.075	0.000	0.871	102.79	6.60	8.40	4.18	29.25	47.87
15 Kansas City	0.791	0.138	0.071	0.000	1.047	97.12	7.71	8.67	6.36	10.57	32.46
16 Jackson	0.936	0.064	0.000	0.000	0.657	97.98	5.98	7.10	5.85	38.49	27.82
17 Dallas	0.999	0.000	0.000	0.000	0.741	96.08	5.02	6.66	4.07	12.35	34.39
18 Phoenix	0.861	0.069	0.000	0.061	0.678	95.58	4.73	9.32	6.28	11.84	18.52
19 Denver	0.584	0.252	0.065	0.071	0.686	98.82	6.79	7.84	7.91	16.98	30.34
20 Portland	0.822	0.178	0.000	0.000	0.474	100.41	7.24	7.80	5.73	9.00	34.50
21 San Francisco	0.999	0.001	0.000	0.000	0.637	112.04	8.99	9.66	7.84	20.38	29.24
22 Long Beach	0.999	0.001	0.000	0.000	0.986	103.77	9.78	9.44	7.29	18.31	34.00
23 Lincoln & Minneapolis	0.914	0.086	0.000	0.000	1.121	98.82	5.00	8.00	4.51	9.27	41.46

Table B.2—continued

VISN	Research Costs Per 1,000 Unique Patients	% of Funded Research	Average Building Age as of 2001	Average Building Condition (scale of 1–5)	Leased Square Feet Per Unique Patient	Ratio of Historic to Total Number of Buildings	Total Number of Buildings	Indicator for Recent Consolidation
01 Boston	119.73	0.016	50.24	2.12	1.49	0.184	46.48	0.454
02 Albany	23.63	0.005	51.91	3.00	0.29	0.511	147.33	0.996
03 Bronx	66.93	0.006	44.20	3.28	0.86	0.283	45.75	0.694
04 Pittsburgh	46.00	0.006	45.80	3.32	0.64	0.118	26.87	0.180
05 Baltimore	90.70	0.018	45.67	3.08	0.68	0.072	97.20	0.439
06 Durham	38.41	0.005	42.88	3.36	0.63	0.224	28.46	0.001
07 Atlanta	62.79	0.009	41.32	3.59	1.35	0.217	23.75	0.123
08 Bay Pines	39.46	0.004	23.11	3.78	1.89	0.093	25.21	0.207
09 Nashville	51.78	0.006	42.57	3.44	0.69	0.273	32.77	0.001
10 Cincinnati	59.00	0.011	45.31	3.29	2.48	0.276	42.74	0.001
11 Ann Arbor	66.14	0.006	45.88	3.19	1.00	0.366	39.41	0.136
12 Chicago	73.39	0.011	51.71	3.26	0.91	0.199	40.73	0.219
15 Kansas City	23.15	0.003	41.11	3.35	0.31	0.197	65.32	0.127
16 Jackson	53.33	0.006	42.22	3.17	0.99	0.180	29.54	0.002
17 Dallas	80.62	0.010	38.47	3.16	1.50	0.299	55.48	0.994
18 Phoenix	48.71	0.005	38.77	3.59	1.01	0.245	29.11	0.003
19 Denver	59.52	0.006	49.33	3.21	1.73	0.239	35.78	0.180
20 Portland	108.85	0.015	46.47	3.09	1.48	0.207	50.99	0.314
21 San Francisco	189.06	0.023	27.90	3.24	1.62	0.060	41.36	0.240
22 Long Beach	164.69	0.026	22.25	3.64	1.71	0.084	56.23	0.316
23 Lincoln & Minneapolis	48.91	0.008	45.68	3.50	0.42	0.198	71.67	0.488

Table B.2—continued

VISN	Occupancy Rate	Number of CBOCs Per 1,000 Unique Patients	Direct Patient Care FTEs Per 1,000 Unique Patients	Non-Patient Care FTEs Per 1,000 Unique Patients	LTC Beds Per 1,000 Unique Patients	Special Program Beds Per 1,000 Unique Patients
01 Boston	0.827	0.200	10.03	32.63	4.44	0.453
02 Albany	1.573	0.416	4.87	13.32	1.88	0.002
03 Bronx	0.946	0.199	10.88	34.61	6.39	0.457
04 Pittsburgh	0.795	0.168	8.00	27.30	6.59	0.002
05 Baltimore	0.828	0.154	11.53	38.77	7.78	0.003
06 Durham	0.806	0.086	9.21	30.81	5.05	0.731
07 Atlanta	0.732	0.082	8.53	32.22	4.00	0.384
08 Bay Pines	0.805	0.101	8.60	26.19	3.16	0.330
09 Nashville	0.815	0.111	9.86	32.78	3.63	0.282
10 Cincinnati	0.689	0.137	10.44	34.80	7.42	0.264
11 Ann Arbor	0.723	0.118	9.00	31.50	4.47	0.002
12 Chicago	0.777	0.149	12.32	36.97	7.92	0.688
15 Kansas City	0.628	0.099	6.74	24.26	3.02	0.100
16 Jackson	0.831	0.079	8.68	29.41	3.11	0.110
17 Dallas	0.780	0.155	9.67	35.94	7.59	0.403
18 Phoenix	0.684	0.161	7.86	24.40	2.79	0.276
19 Denver	0.898	0.236	8.35	25.54	2.21	0.002
20 Portland	0.767	0.096	10.04	33.23	7.18	0.338
21 San Francisco	0.797	0.135	9.45	28.32	4.98	0.387
22 Long Beach	0.755	0.121	10.36	31.19	4.51	0.641
23 Lincoln & Minneapolis	1.075	0.203	6.99	22.18	3.66	0.002

Supplemental Regression and Simulation Model Results

Tables C.1–C.12 contain findings from the regression, simulation, and disaggregation analyses not presented in Chapter Three. These findings include the results of analyses that included Basic Care Priority 7 patients and the results for the all variables models (some tables exclude, while other include, Basic Care Priority 7s).

Table C.1
Regression Results for the Base and Selected Variables Regression Models, Including Basic Care Priority 7s

Variable Category		Base Regression Model (VERA-10) 0.46[a]		Selected Variables Regression Model (VERA-10) 0.49[a]		Selected Variables Regression Model with VA DCGs 0.62[a]	
		Estimate	t-Statistic	Estimate	t-Statistic	Estimate	t-Statistic
Intercept		-2116.13	-1.95	-3427.90	-3.26 **	-3651.81	-3.13 **
Patient characteristics							
Age	Less than 25			Reference		Reference	
	25–34			256.78	4.77 **	457.29	8.76 **
	35–44			651.09	10.56 **	717.35	11.11 **
	45–54			1148.58	17.95 **	1021.05	15.06 **
	55–64			1496.05	21.64 **	1155.62	16.09 **
	65–74			572.13	7.72 **	584.55	7.73 **
	75–84			701.88	9.23 **	446.63	5.76 **
	85 and over			749.89	8.55 **	124.46	1.49
Gender	Female			146.61	3.29 **	-302.79	-9.41 **
	Male			Reference		Reference	
Physicians per capita	Less than 0.001			Reference		Reference	
	0.001 to 0.002			-176.90	-2.58 *	0.37	0.01
	0.0021 to 0.003			-148.56	-2.46 *	13.46	0.24
	Greater than 0.003			24.32	0.35	81.29	1.26
Hospital beds per capita	Less than 0.003			Reference		Reference	
	0.003 to 0.006			-197.45	-3.01 **	-90.94	-1.36
	Greater than 0.006			-184.17	-3.08 **	-63.95	-1.01
Rural or urban status	Urban			Reference		Reference	
	Suburban			125.97	1.69	100.31	1.65
	Rural			1.93	0.03	10.33	0.21
	Very rural			-58.21	-1.31	-72.37	-1.78
Distance to closest facility				1.44	1.77	2.46	3.80 **
Distance to closest CBOC				5.37	4.11 **	1.63	1.26

Table C.1—continued

Variable Category		Base Regression Model (VERA-10) 0.46[a]		Selected Variables Regression Model (VERA-10) 0.49[a]		Selected Variables Regression Model with VA DCGs 0.62[a]	
		Estimate	t-Statistic	Estimate	t-Statistic	Estimate	t-Statistic
Medicare reliance	Not eligible			Reference		Reference	
	No reliance			2632.58	35.23 **	1452.48	29.97 **
	FFS—1 to 24%			3958.78	38.62 **	2116.84	34.87 **
	FFS—25 to 49%			1004.12	19.88 **	286.65	7.86 **
	FFS—50 to 74%			138.35	3.07 **	−236.26	−5.73 **
	FFS—75 to 100%			−784.06	−13.71 **	−692.05	−17.08 **
	HMO—1 to 24%			24411.93	34.76 **	17797.40	22.95 **
	HMO—25 to 49%			7529.60	21.02 **	3557.85	11.87 **
	HMO—50 to 74%			1684.06	17.55 **	558.35	5.98 **
	HMO—75 to 100%			−768.19	−10.85 **	−411.64	−7.45 **
Medicaid generosity for LTC				−0.001	−0.10	0.01	0.84
VERA-10 patient category							
1	Non-Reliant	Reference		Reference			
2	Basic Medical	1,828.61	30.71 **	1,393.36	22.58 **		
3	Mental Health	3,231.00	47.20 **	2,495.79	35.18 **		
4	Heart, Lung, and GI	2,731.87	29.18 **	2,142.60	28.38 **		
5	Oncology	6,351.01	41.09 **	5,470.41	41.06 **		
6	Multiple Problem	15,455.32	59.12 **	13,755.65	59.00 **		
7	Specialized Care	15,958.43	52.50 **	14,283.25	51.98 **		
8	Supportive Care	22,608.68	52.69 **	20,475.00	51.61 **		
9	Chronic Mental Illness	29,738.11	49.74 **	27,790.24	47.03 **		
10	Critically Ill	53,479.27	111.75 **	50,318.38	114.85 **		
VA DCG patient category							
	DCG 0.1					Reference	
	DCG 0.2					396.43	20.95 **
	DCG 0.3					705.22	28.20 **
	DCG 0.4					509.97	20.53 **
	DCG 0.5					841.03	29.57 **
	DCG 0.7					962.65	33.03 **
	DCG 1					1,453.66	36.74 **
	DCG 1.5					1,961.28	40.01 **
	DCG 2					2,378.45	39.15 **

Table C.1—continued

Variable Category		Base Regression Model (VERA-10) 0.46[a]		Selected Variables Regression Model (VERA-10) 0.49[a]		Selected Variables Regression Model with VA DCGs 0.62[a]	
		Estimate	t–Statistic	Estimate	t–Statistic	Estimate	t–Statistic
	DCG 2.5					2,645.43	41.01 **
	DCG 3					3,496.13	40.89 **
	DCG 4					4,480.08	39.28 **
	DCG 5					5,771.21	43.29 **
	DCG 6					8,176.98	48.66 **
	DCG 7.5					12,603.85	53.48 **
	DCG 10					22,941.83	66.92 **
	DCG 15					35,239.22	73.09 **
	DCG 20					42,107.23	83.57 **
	DCG 25					48,041.85	97.80 **
	DCG 30					54,025.52	115.16 **
	DCG 40					60,530.42	149.22 **
	DCG 50					62,601.67	121.07 **
	DCG 60					64,945.71	142.33 **
	DCG 70					65,228.14	106.55 **
Facility characteristics							
Rural or urban status of facility	Urban			11.54	0.07	-164.27	-0.88
	Suburban			-280.24	-1.61	-452.32	-2.36 *
	Rural			-290.03	-1.25	-342.45	-1.54
	Very rural			Reference		Reference	
Residents per full-time MD		352.70	3.70 **	161.98	2.13 *	-90.55	-1.13
VA labor index		19.62	1.81	21.61	1.94	27.98	2.34 *
Average food cost per bed day				19.68	1.36	4.85	0.35
Energy price (dollars per million Btus)				-12.93	-0.53	17.93	0.64
Contract labor costs				-2.48	-0.19	3.17	0.22
Square feet of building space per acre of land				3.51	2.44 *	4.72	4.53 **
Square feet of building space per unique patient				7.56	2.91 **	8.62	2.75 **
Research costs per unique patient		3.66	6.41 **	3.44	6.13 **	3.35	5.72 **

NOTES: * indicates significance at the 95% level and ** at the 99% level. Robust t–statistics are calculated by clustering data at the facility level.
[a]R-squared.

Table C.2
Comparison of Actual and Simulated Allocations from the Base and Selected Variables Regression Models, Including Basic Care Priority 7s

VISN	VERA FY 03 Actual Allocation	Base Regression Model		Selected Variables Model with VERA-10		Selected Variables Model with VA DCGs	
		Simulated Allocation	% diff FY 03	Simulated Allocation	% diff FY 03	Simulated Allocation	% diff FY 03
01 Boston	1,012,354	1,056,309	4.3%	1,032,845	2.0%	1,002,462	−1.0%
02 Albany	556,418	575,758	3.5%	587,424	5.6%	589,893	6.0%
03 Bronx	1,111,597	1,111,420	0.0%	1,086,958	−2.2%	1,093,058	−1.7%
04 Pittsburgh	1,076,519	1,119,119	4.0%	1,055,796	−1.9%	975,509	−9.4%
05 Baltimore	617,523	594,717	−3.7%	588,889	−4.6%	575,466	−6.8%
06 Durham	990,671	960,553	−3.0%	978,706	−1.2%	952,923	−3.8%
07 Atlanta	1,158,656	1,130,577	−2.4%	1,158,475	0.0%	1,155,011	−0.3%
08 Bay Pines	1,655,761	1,720,476	3.9%	1,649,817	−0.4%	1,656,139	0.0%
09 Nashville	926,758	931,436	0.5%	950,127	2.5%	968,545	4.5%
10 Cincinnati	771,274	748,949	−2.9%	719,501	−6.7%	735,060	−4.7%
11 Ann Arbor	849,127	850,405	0.2%	860,593	1.4%	842,825	−0.7%
12 Chicago	978,050	981,358	0.3%	998,781	2.1%	1,016,495	3.9%
15 Kansas City	761,453	738,673	−3.0%	728,896	−4.3%	751,466	−1.3%
16 Jackson	1,688,502	1,598,637	−5.3%	1,682,505	−0.4%	1,646,252	−2.5%
17 Dallas	936,733	909,684	−2.9%	909,004	−3.0%	882,969	−5.7%
18 Phoenix	803,265	821,635	2.3%	820,176	2.1%	846,592	5.4%
19 Denver	528,463	520,636	−1.5%	527,057	−0.3%	592,179	12.1%
20 Portland	902,764	872,276	−3.4%	891,908	−1.2%	942,075	4.4%
21 San Francisco	1,062,177	1,066,032	0.4%	1,090,743	2.7%	1,099,869	3.5%
22 Long Beach	1,219,641	1,210,171	−0.8%	1,175,542	−3.6%	1,150,434	−5.7%
23 Lincoln & Minneapolis	917,822	1,006,707	9.7%	1,031,785	12.4%	1,050,307	14.4%
Total amount redistributed		290,983		266,502		430,617	
% of FY 03 dollars redistributed		1.4%		1.3%		2.1%	

NOTE: Figures shown are in thousands of dollars.

Table C.3
Disaggregation of Simulated Allocations from the Selected Variables Model with VERA-10, Including Basic Care Priority 7s

	VISN 1	VISN 2	VISN 3	VISN 4	VISN 5	VISN 6	VISN 7	VISN 8
(1) Simulated allocations from SVM with VERA-10	1,032,845	587,424	1,086,958	1,055,796	588,889	978,706	1,158,475	1,649,817
(2) Unadjusted average allocation	982,277	606,669	1,047,663	1,177,746	516,972	979,348	1,181,266	1,896,603
(3) Difference (1)–(2)	50,568	–19,245	39,294	–121,950	71,917	–642	–22,791	–246,787
Patient characteristics								
(4) Age	–3,879	–4,685	–9,400	–7,245		3,065	4,849	–4,305
(5) Gender	–487	–30	–638	–1,053	93	223	332	–436
(6) Physicians per capita	8,269	–662	15,160	669	2,975	–7,422	–5,766	4,407
(7) Hospital beds per capita	–2,863	–448	–652	2,021	3,270	955	2,121	1,664
(8) Rural or urban status	851	622	7,649	2,189	1,946	–1,677	–2,015	8,994
(9) Distance to closest facility	–4,821	3,686	–8,894	–7,023	–3,474	–2,382	715	–9
(10) Distance to closest CBOC	–10,688	–8,859	–20,134	–13,094	–8,144	20,195	12,847	–19,338
(11) Medicare reliance	7,372	9,643	–33,858	–35,871	–395	6,437	–6,200	–33,199
(12) Medicaid generosity for LTC	–1,459	–839	–1,101	–1,160	250	764	833	1,259
(13) VERA-10 health status measure	20,568	–534	32,659	–18,615	57,734	25,061	–31,072	–56,911
Facility characteristics								
(14) Rural or urban status	–9,559	3,289	5,215	1,244	2,703	1,185	175	10,450
(15) Residents per full-time MD	–76	–645	–426	–5,522	–278	–4,903	776	–14,681
(16) VA labor index	12,701	–5,383	37,260	–2,456	8,962	–10,046	–11,716	–42,422
(17) Average food cost per bed day	814	–8,962	–5,404	–915	–351	–1,656	–1,082	–688
(18) Energy price ($/million Btus)	–4,168	–2,231	–2,672	10	–2,733	–1,388	1,469	–7,110
(19) Contract labor cost share	–296	1,757	1,007	–561	–386	855	–83	589
(20) Square feet of building space per acre of land	–6,678	–4,148	–757	–2,739	–3,023	–3,100	22,015	1,253
(21) Square feet of building space per unique patient	8,040	21,196	26,771	–9,540	4,872	–2,696	–4,100	–49,926
(22) Research costs per 1,000 unique patients	36,927	–22,014	–2,492	–22,287	7,897	–24,112	–6,890	–46,376
Sum of differences—rows (4) through (22)	50,568	–19,245	39,294	–121,950	71,917	–642	–22,791	–246,785

Table C.3—continued

	VISN 9	VISN 10	VISN 11	VISN 12	VISN 15	VISN 16	VISN 17	VISN 18
(1) Simulated allocations from SVM with VERA-10	950,127	719,501	860,593	998,781	728,896	1,682,505	909,004	820,176
(2) Unadjusted average allocation	967,279	686,732	867,636	876,677	770,012	1,709,170	904,688	948,652
(3) Difference (1)–(2)	–17,152	32,769	–7,043	122,105	–41,116	–26,665	4,316	–128,477
Patient characteristics								
(4) Age	1,216	–125	–1,298	–4,738	351	11,636	5,006	–2,201
(5) Gender	287	–313	–292	–96	–691	–519	643	1,601
(6) Physicians per capita	–7,739	–2,097	–1,747	1,487	–6,440	–3,819	–1,186	1,553
(7) Hospital beds per capita	1,981	–2,624	–2,324	–2,557	3,978	5,979	–650	–1,962
(8) Rural or urban status	–5,367	1,443	–580	536	–6,406	–4,550	825	–338
(9) Distance to closest facility	149	–3,280	412	–1,819	965	3,933	2,946	2,834
(10) Distance to closest CBOC	3,073	–8,600	3,056	–8,010	900	38,988	–2,697	14,403
(11) Medicare reliance	20,459	–6,731	405	17,244	18,498	7,002	–6,786	12,354
(12) Medicaid generosity for LTC	–32	–1,399	–302	–493	–146	1,674	870	1,342
(13) VERA-10 health status measure	–21,266	65,408	–6,739	76,113	–13,852	–62,767	11,131	–81,567
Facility characteristics								
(14) Rural or urban status	5,289	–1,144	–11,347	–4,681	–6,680	2,098	4,916	678
(15) Residents per full-time MD	5,964	–1,751	–3,636	4,751	9,531	–3,728	810	–1,383
(16) VA labor index	–12,403	975	1,121	12,697	–9,885	–14,460	–16,004	–19,580
(17) Average food cost per bed day	5,426	–3,310	3,418	756	4,593	–3,206	–5,557	–7,253
(18) Energy price ($/million Btus)	1,684	395	2,112	829	160	8,291	5,522	–1,641
(19) Contract labor cost share	690	–593	–61	566	–432	–451	666	–493
(20) Square feet of building space per acre of land	–4,695	–1,672	4,870	6,468	–5,607	26,002	–5,174	–5,970
(21) Square feet of building space per unique patient	2,384	4,141	8,646	21,016	–1,061	–15,983	1,768	–24,533
(22) Research costs per 1,000 unique patients	–14,250	–5,954	–2,759	2,034	–28,891	–22,786	7,269	–16,321
Sum of differences—rows (4) through (22)	–17,152	32,769	–7,043	122,104	–41,115	–26,665	4,316	–128,476

Table C.3—continued

	VISN 19	VISN 20	VISN 21	VISN 22	VISN 23
(1) Simulated allocations from SVM with VERA-10	527,057	891,908	1,090,743	1,175,542	1,031,785
(2) Unadjusted average allocation	550,889	829,897	932,075	1,062,980	1,030,298
(3) Difference (1)–(2)	–23,832	62,011	158,669	112,562	1,487
Patient characteristics					
(4) Age	1,642	6,343	5,831	5,674	–7,739
(5) Gender	45	506	879	352	–404
(6) Physicians per capita	–89	–2,271	4,479	7,561	–7,321
(7) Hospital beds per capita	–390	–3,493	–3,661	–5,015	4,668
(8) Rural or urban status	–4,039	–1,971	3,362	8,318	–9,793
(9) Distance to closest facility	4,728	–468	3,244	–1,226	9,781
(10) Distance to closest CBOC	1,088	5,650	–1,090	–16,027	16,481
(11) Medicare reliance	12,289	15,101	1,825	–37,667	32,078
(12) Medicaid generosity for LTC	–285	–108	567	845	–1,080
(13) VERA-10 health status measure	–20,119	27,508	3,077	25,097	–30,913
Facility characteristics					
(14) Rural or urban status	–8,818	–5,179	4,842	5,565	–241
(15) Residents per full-time MD	–627	–7,301	–2,607	10,181	15,552
(16) VA labor index	–2,351	2,900	54,030	20,561	–4,500
(17) Average food cost per bed day	959	3,091	10,339	15,519	–6,532
(18) Energy price ($/million Btus)	1,455	2,265	–2,414	–2,100	2,265
(19) Contract labor cost share	–788	–160	–1,236	–1,105	514
(20) Square feet of building space per acre of land	–1,140	–6,892	584	–1,019	–8,579
(21) Square feet of building space per unique patient	–2,748	1,753	–6,125	1,356	14,768
(22) Research costs per 1,000 unique patients	–4,645	24,736	82,741	75,691	–17,518
Sum of differences—rows (4) through (22)	–23,832	62,011	158,668	112,562	1,487

NOTE: Figures shown are in thousands of dollars.

Table C.4
Disaggregation of Simulated Allocations from the Selected Variables Model with VA DCGs, Including Basic Care Priority 7s

	VISN 1	VISN 2	VISN 3	VISN 4	VISN 5	VISN 6	VISN 7	VISN 8
(1) Simulated allocations from SVM with VA DCGs	1,002,462	589,893	1,093,058	975,509	575,466	952,923	1,155,011	1,656,139
(2) Unadjusted average allocation	982,277	606,669	1,047,663	1,177,746	516,972	979,348	1,181,266	1,896,603
(3) Difference (1)–(2)	20,185	–16,776	45,395	–202,237	58,494	–26,426	–26,255	–240,464
Patient characteristics								
(4) Age	–5,653	–4,543	–11,363	–8,822	895	5,576	7,590	–8,314
(5) Gender	1,006	63	1,317	2,175	–191	–460	–686	900
(6) Physicians per capita	63	–1,568	2,958	110	960	–1,476	–1,648	3,733
(7) Hospital beds per capita	–1,098	417	786	1,294	580	–14	549	2,019
(8) Rural or urban status	722	717	6,201	1,950	1,614	–1,176	–1,291	7,439
(9) Distance to closest facility	–8,230	6,293	–15,182	–11,989	–5,931	–4,067	1,221	–15
(10) Distance to closest CBOC	–3,256	–2,699	–6,134	–3,989	–2,481	6,152	3,914	–5,891
(11) Medicare reliance	3,376	4,771	–21,373	–21,308	790	2,971	–5,389	–19,396
(12) Medicaid generosity for LTC	11,557	6,643	8,722	9,187	–1,977	–6,052	–6,600	–9,973
(13) VA DCG health status measure	–29,739	–18,865	–1,689	–135,375	36,757	12,202	–23,759	–81,754
Facility characteristics								
(14) Rural or urban status	–7,595	2,852	4,514	448	2,339	526	–606	9,045
(15) Residents per full-time MD	43	360	238	3,087	156	2,741	–434	8,207
(16) VA labor index	16,443	–6,969	48,238	–3,179	11,603	–13,006	–15,168	–54,921
(17) Average food cost per bed day	201	–2,208	–1,332	–225	–87	–408	–267	–170
(18) Energy price ($/million Btus)	5,777	3,092	3,703	–13	3,788	1,924	–2,036	9,856
(19) Contract labor cost share	379	–2,246	–1,287	717	493	–1,093	107	–753
(20) Square feet of building space per acre of land	–8,992	–5,586	–1,019	–3,688	–4,070	–4,174	29,643	1,688
(21) Square feet of building space per unique patient	9,168	24,170	30,526	–10,878	5,555	–3,075	–4,675	–56,930
(22) Research costs per 1,000 unique patients	36,014	–21,470	–2,430	–21,736	7,702	–23,517	–6,719	–45,230
Sum of differences—rows (4) through (22)	20,185	–16,776	45,395	–202,237	58,494	–26,425	–26,255	–240,463

Table C.4—continued

	VISN 9	VISN 10	VISN 11	VISN 12	VISN 15	VISN 16	VISN 17	VISN 18
(1) Simulated allocations from SVM with VA DCGs	968,545	735,060	842,825	1,016,495	751,466	1,646,252	882,969	846,592
(2) Unadjusted average allocation	967,279	686,732	867,636	876,677	770,012	1,709,170	904,688	948,652
(3) Difference (1)–(2)	1,267	48,328	–24,811	139,818	–18,546	–62,917	–21,720	–102,060
Patient characteristics								
(4) Age	3,078	428	–1,031	–4,683	–585	11,157	5,952	–1,031
(5) Gender	–592	647	604	198	1,428	1,073	–1,328	–3,306
(6) Physicians per capita	–4,083	–1,903	–5	–2,617	–987	–2,158	–1	–148
(7) Hospital beds per capita	915	–945	–739	–216	1,533	2,691	–332	–1,506
(8) Rural or urban status	–4,672	1,253	–334	377	–5,620	–3,776	711	–159
(9) Distance to closest facility	255	–5,598	703	–3,104	1,647	6,714	5,029	4,837
(10) Distance to closest CBOC	936	–2,620	931	–2,440	274	11,877	–822	4,388
(11) Medicare reliance	10,376	–3,644	–2,301	8,886	7,869	3,933	–1,131	9,835
(12) Medicaid generosity for LTC	254	11,079	2,392	3,901	1,156	–13,260	–6,889	–10,632
(13) VA DCG health status measure	28,983	51,000	–28,468	96,252	33,949	–48,327	1,724	–31,659
Facility characteristics								
(14) Rural or urban status	4,588	332	–11,765	–3,488	–5,608	936	4,273	2,711
(15) Residents per full-time MD	–3,334	979	2,032	–2,656	–5,328	2,084	–453	773
(16) VA labor index	–16,057	1,262	1,451	16,438	–12,798	–18,720	–20,719	–25,349
(17) Average food cost per bed day	1,337	–816	842	186	1,132	–790	–1,369	–1,787
(18) Energy price ($/million Btus)	–2,334	–548	–2,928	–1,149	–221	–11,492	–7,653	2,275
(19) Contract labor cost share	–882	758	78	–723	552	576	–851	630
(20) Square feet of building space per acre of land	–6,322	–2,252	6,557	8,710	–7,550	35,011	–6,967	–8,039
(21) Square feet of building space per unique patient	2,719	4,722	9,859	23,964	–1,210	–18,225	2,016	–27,975
(22) Research costs per 1,000 unique patients	–13,898	–5,807	–2,691	1,984	–28,177	–22,223	7,089	–15,918
Sum of differences—rows (4) through (22)	1,267	48,328	–24,811	139,818	–18,546	–62,917	–21,720	–102,060

Table C.4—continued

	VISN 19	VISN 20	VISN 21	VISN 22	VISN 23
(1) Simulated allocations from SVM with VA DCGs	592,179	942,075	1,099,869	1,150,434	1,050,307
(2) Unadjusted average allocation	550,889	829,897	932,075	1,062,980	1,030,298
(3) Difference (1)–(2)	41,290	112,178	167,795	87,454	20,009
Patient characteristics					
(4) Age	1,662	6,928	4,190	6,898	–8,329
(5) Gender	–94	–1,045	–1,815	–727	833
(6) Physicians per capita	985	490	1,888	7,297	–1,890
(7) Hospital beds per capita	–656	–2,100	–2,621	–2,915	2,359
(8) Rural or urban status	–3,618	–1,510	2,880	6,707	–8,415
(9) Distance to closest facility	8,071	–798	5,538	–2,093	16,697
(10) Distance to closest CBOC	331	1,721	–332	–4,883	5,021
(11) Medicare reliance	6,839	11,573	4,560	–15,104	13,868
(12) Medicaid generosity for LTC	2,259	859	–4,488	–6,689	8,552
(13) VA DCG health status measure	44,091	79,209	427	–8,924	23,965
Facility characteristics					
(14) Rural or urban status	–5,917	–5,655	4,187	4,814	–929
(15) Residents per full-time MD	351	4,082	1,457	–5,691	–8,694
(16) VA labor index	–3,043	3,754	69,949	26,619	–5,826
(17) Average food cost per bed day	236	762	2,548	3,824	–1,609
(18) Energy price ($/million Btus)	–2,016	–3,140	3,346	2,911	–3,139
(19) Contract labor cost share	1,007	205	1,580	1,412	–657
(20) Square feet of building space per acre of land	–1,534	–9,280	786	–1,372	–11,551
(21) Square feet of building space per unique patient	–3,134	1,999	–6,984	1,547	16,839
(22) Research costs per 1,000 unique patients	–4,530	24,125	80,697	73,820	–17,085
(23) Sum of differences—rows (4) through (22)	41,290	112,177	167,793	87,453	20,009

NOTE: Figures shown are in thousands of dollars.

Table C.5
Regression Results for the All Variables Regression Models, Excluding Basic Care Priority 7s

Variable Category		Base Regression Model (VERA-10) 0.46[a]		Selected Variables Model with VERA-10 0.50[a]		Selected Variables Model with VA DCGs 0.62[a]	
		Estimate	t-Statistic	Estimate	t-Statistic	Estimate	t-Statistic
Intercept		-3682.89	-2.56 *	-5618.46	-4.50 **	-4080.63	-2.95 **
Patient characteristics							
Age	Less than 25			Reference		Reference	
	25–34			71.17	1.91	66.50	1.32
	35–44			506.00	11.22 **	279.38	4.50 **
	45–54			1061.46	22.51 **	578.87	9.72 **
	55–64			1675.27	28.10 **	851.64	13.62 **
	65–74			1136.73	17.98 **	490.90	7.24 **
	75–84			1109.58	16.33 **	239.11	3.32 **
	85 and over			942.06	10.58 **	-191.74	-2.24 *
Income	Missing			394.38	7.47 **	14.33	0.39
	$20,000 or less			186.44	4.93 **	-176.24	-4.89 **
	$21,000–$40,000			267.44	6.64 **	-19.39	-0.55
	$41,000–$60,000			-55.50	-1.77	-51.11	-1.61
	$61,000–$80,000			21.16	0.36	22.65	0.39
	More than $80,000			Reference		Reference	
Race/ethnicity	Hispanic			-776.78	-4.26 **	-479.08	-3.51 **
	American Indian			-327.77	-2.07 *	-474.36	-2.86 **
	Black			-202.75	-2.88 **	-126.52	-2.10 *
	Asian			-1199.81	-3.36 **	-944.26	-1.97 *
	White			Reference		Reference	
Gender	Female			510.78	12.36 **	544.28	14.45 **
	Male			Reference		Reference	
Marital status	Single			391.63	19.49 **	98.24	5.32 **
	Married			Reference		Reference	
Physicians per capita	Less than 0.001			-189.26	-2.56 *	-8.99	-0.14
	0.001 to 0.002			-170.49	-2.36 *	-21.52	-0.31
	0.0021 to 0.003			28.62	0.40	56.88	0.94
	Greater than 0.003			Reference		Reference	

Table C.5—continued

Variable Category	Base Regression Model (VERA-10) 0.46[a]		Selected Variables Model with VERA-10 0.50[a]		Selected Variables Model with VA DCGs 0.62[a]	
	Estimate	t-Statistic	Estimate	t-Statistic	Estimate	t-Statistic
Hospital beds per capita						
Less than 0.003			-261.87	-3.71 **	-202.34	-2.93 **
0.003 to 0.006			-203.98	-3.17 **	-103.49	-1.67
Greater than 0.006			Reference		Reference	
Rural or urban status						
Urban			136.36	1.95	114.91	1.95
Suburban			15.08	0.28	36.97	0.74
Rural			-44.65	-0.99	-53.98	-1.32
Very rural			Reference		Reference	
Distance to closest facility			1.70	1.94	2.12	2.87 **
Distance to closest CBOC			7.33	5.91 **	3.89	3.30 **
Priority Group						
1			2045.56	43.15 **	1269.34	29.35 **
2			769.64	26.34 **	495.56	19.35 **
3			501.27	16.67 **	333.64	13.28 **
4			3442.60	35.80 **	1819.22	21.02 **
5			573.20	19.94 **	226.39	9.68 **
6			-142.36	-4.32 **	-65.92	-2.38 *
7			Reference		Reference	
Medicare reliance						
Not eligible			Reference		Reference	
No reliance			1904.92	31.26 **	1032.71	24.96 **
FFS—1 to 24%			3375.51	37.75 **	1765.96	33.55 **
FFS—25 to 49%			440.29	9.54 **	-126.86	-3.38 **
FFS—50 to 74%			-483.08	-9.23 **	-711.00	-15.01 **
FFS—75 to 100%			-1556.96	-23.28 **	-1193.46	-25.61 **
HMO—1 to 24%			23563.98	34.15 **	17313.34	22.73 **
HMO—25 to 49%			6625.75	18.95 **	3015.09	10.26 **
HMO—50 to 74%			865.52	8.82 **	25.93	0.28
HMO—75 to 100%			-1425.42	-16.92 **	-839.94	-12.71 **
Medicaid generosity (general)			0.04	1.28	0.06	1.50
Medicaid generosity for LTC			-0.01	-0.77	-0.01	-0.73
VERA-10 patient category						
1	Reference		Reference			
2	2,073.32	34.03 **	1,575.29	26.43 **		
3	3,292.75	42.28 **	2,288.74	28.38 **		

Table C.5—continued

Variable Category	Base Regression Model (VERA-10) 0.46[a]		Selected Variables Model with VERA-10 0.50[a]		Selected Variables Model with VA DCGs 0.62[a]	
	Estimate	t-Statistic	Estimate	t-Statistic	Estimate	t-Statistic
4 Heart, Lung, and GI	3,125.87	31.50 **	2,488.96	32.08 **		
5 Oncology	6,735.25	42.16 **	5,716.12	44.70 **		
6 Multiple Problem	15,469.82	58.37 **	13,393.90	60.83 **		
7 Specialized Care	15,846.65	52.69 **	13,757.60	49.72 **		
8 Supportive Care	22,507.05	53.06 **	19,485.86	50.07 **		
9 Chronic Mental Illness	29,631.93	49.93 **	26,600.09	45.81 **		
10 Critically Ill	53,377.39	112.02 **	49,165.20	112.80 **		
VA DCG patient category						
DCG 0.1					Reference	
DCG 0.2					443.78	23.49 **
DCG 0.3					772.77	34.52 **
DCG 0.4					559.85	21.48 **
DCG 0.5					933.37	33.47 **
DCG 0.7					981.76	35.99 **
DCG 1					1,503.54	41.39 **
DCG 1.5					1,999.29	44.06 **
DCG 2					2,404.21	42.54 **
DCG 2.5					2,640.66	43.52 **
DCG 3					3,457.85	43.13 **
DCG 4					4,438.23	39.90 **
DCG 5					5,703.53	43.99 **
DCG 6					8,039.96	49.36 **
DCG 7.5					12,345.15	52.81 **
DCG 10					22,490.24	67.39 **
DCG 15					34,592.16	74.77 **
DCG 20					41,450.82	83.97 **
DCG 25					47,371.50	97.32 **
DCG 30					53,324.17	113.93 **
DCG 40					59,791.87	147.73 **
DCG 50					61,865.77	120.53 **
DCG 60					64,106.30	137.28 **
DCG 70					64,420.50	103.03 **

Table C.5—continued

Variable Category		Base Regression Model (VERA-10) 0.46[a]		Selected Variables Model with VERA-10 0.50[a]		Selected Variables Model with VA DCGs 0.62[a]	
		Estimate	t-Statistic	Estimate	t-Statistic	Estimate	t-Statistic
Facility characteristics							
Rural or urban status of facility	Urban			−299.77	−1.25	−542.54	−2.60 **
	Suburban			−479.84	−2.00	−746.87	−3.67 **
	Rural			−492.84	−1.73	−597.89	−2.51 *
	Very rural			Reference		Reference	
Residents per full-time MD		432.91	3.63 **	184.85	2.51 *	−79.76	−0.82
VA labor index		35.41	2.46 *	32.38	2.56 *	36.83	2.52 *
Average food cost per bed day				20.68	1.40	13.35	0.77
Energy price (dollars per million Btus)				−23.63	−0.87	14.14	0.49
Contract labor costs				−1.29	−0.08	8.52	0.48
Square feet of building space per acre of land				1.48	0.90	3.48	3.08 **
Square feet of building space per unique patient				11.94	2.05 *	12.33	1.87
Research costs per unique patient		4.07	5.76 **	2.14	2.60 *	1.14	1.29
Percentage of funded research				4189.32	0.70	17443.24	2.94 **
Average building age as of 2001				−8.13	−2.39 *	−5.30	−1.30
Average building condition (scale of 1–5)				−5.85	−0.10	−49.00	−0.75
Leased square feet per patient				80.50	1.43	72.05	1.23
Ratio of historic to total number of buildings				153.09	0.78	164.97	0.74
Total number of buildings				−0.48	−0.30	−2.14	−1.22
Indicator for recent facility/management consolidation				39.40	0.42	162.56	1.44
Occupancy rate				−85.51	−0.44	−155.21	−0.65
Number of CBOCs per 1,000 unique patients				798.26	2.41 *	651.98	1.45
Direct patient care FTEs per 1,000 unique patients				95.70	2.92 **	38.93	1.05
Non-patient care FTEs per 1,000 unique patients				−9.84	−0.95	0.37	0.03
LTC beds per 1,000 unique patients				−7.90	−0.80	−5.53	−0.29
Special program beds per 1,000 unique patients				−64.65	−1.03	−28.30	−0.45

NOTE: * indicates significance at the 95% level and ** at the 99% level. Robust t-statistics are calculated by clustering data at the facility level.
[a] R-squared.

Table C.6
Comparison of Actual and Simulated Allocations from the Base and All Variables Models, Excluding Basic Care Priority 7s

VISN	VERA FY 03 Actual Allocation	Base Regression Model Simulated Allocation	Base Regression Model % diff FY 03	Selected Variables Model with VERA-10 Simulated Allocation	Selected Variables Model with VERA-10 % diff FY 03	Selected Variables Model with VA DCGs Simulated Allocation	Selected Variables Model with VA DCGs % diff FY 03
01 Boston	1,012,354	1,026,815	1.4%	1,045,801	3.3%	1,032,708	2.0%
02 Albany	556,418	555,058	−0.2%	575,312	3.4%	573,868	3.1%
03 Bronx	1,111,597	1,052,198	−5.3%	1,050,983	−5.5%	1,065,623	−4.1%
04 Pittsburgh	1,076,519	1,090,602	1.3%	1,003,049	−6.8%	944,784	−12.2%
05 Baltimore	617,523	619,825	0.4%	610,965	−1.1%	599,771	−2.9%
06 Durham	990,671	985,498	−0.5%	992,395	0.2%	966,171	−2.5%
07 Atlanta	1,158,656	1,159,770	0.1%	1,147,582	−1.0%	1,162,053	0.3%
08 Bay Pines	1,655,761	1,683,309	1.7%	1,646,522	−0.6%	1,648,410	−0.4%
09 Nashville	926,758	936,261	1.0%	970,072	4.7%	974,684	5.2%
10 Cincinnati	771,274	772,437	0.2%	756,284	−1.9%	755,660	−2.0%
11 Ann Arbor	849,127	841,891	−0.9%	846,787	−0.3%	827,256	−2.6%
12 Chicago	978,050	971,537	−0.7%	1,009,520	3.2%	1,014,321	3.7%
15 Kansas City	761,453	728,287	−4.4%	696,657	−8.5%	728,431	−4.3%
16 Jackson	1,688,502	1,660,811	−1.6%	1,713,279	1.5%	1,671,058	−1.0%
17 Dallas	936,733	935,714	−0.1%	937,036	0.0%	929,583	−0.8%
18 Phoenix	803,265	791,490	−1.5%	784,063	−2.4%	802,436	−0.1%
19 Denver	528,463	522,899	−1.1%	537,276	1.7%	589,931	11.6%
20 Portland	902,764	920,155	1.9%	944,290	4.6%	976,334	8.1%
21 San Francisco	1,062,177	1,079,743	1.7%	1,071,066	0.8%	1,078,942	1.6%
22 Long Beach	1,219,641	1,251,681	2.6%	1,215,905	−0.3%	1,186,340	−2.7%
23 Lincoln & Minneapolis	917,822	939,546	2.4%	970,685	5.8%	997,165	8.6%
Total amount redistributed		158,897		266,020		356,544	
% of FY 03 dollars redistributed		0.8%		1.3%		1.7%	

NOTE: Figures shown are in thousands of dollars.

Table C.7
Disaggregation of Simulated Allocations from the All Variables Model with VERA-10, Excluding Basic Care Priority 7s

		VISN 1	VISN 2	VISN 3	VISN 4	VISN 5	VISN 6	VISN 7	VISN 8
(1)	Simulated allocations from AVM with VERA-10	1,045,801	575,312	1,050,983	1,003,049	610,965	992,395	1,147,582	1,646,522
(2)	Unadjusted average allocation	947,153	567,019	917,287	1,131,336	544,274	1,021,624	1,231,463	1,874,403
(3)	Difference (1)–(2)	98,648	8,294	133,695	−128,287	66,690	−29,229	−83,881	−227,881
	Patient characteristics								
(4)	Age	2,518	−1,299	2,055	3,876	−2,910	−2,961	−3,676	6,857
(5)	Income	−438	762	1,666	26	349	−1,116	−10	−1,874
(6)	Race	10,625	6,606	−5,090	9,920	−1,169	3,541	1,386	−37,317
(7)	Gender	−665	−269	−1,554	−1,304	646	1,174	1,315	−361
(8)	Martial status	1,313	277	4,257	−1,642	3,092	−3,313	−2,682	−7,904
(9)	Physicians per capita	7,262	−337	12,300	884	3,433	−7,413	−5,473	2,520
(10)	Hospital beds per capita	−2,312	747	1,280	3,090	2,204	−425	1,423	3,816
(11)	Rural or urban status	892	331	5,448	1,624	1,822	−1,625	−1,686	7,099
(12)	Distance to closest facility	−4,489	3,123	−7,766	−6,790	−3,800	−2,075	898	72
(13)	Distance to closest CBOC	−11,744	−9,254	−19,799	−13,928	−9,929	23,342	14,612	−19,849
(14)	Priority status	8,661	−9,780	−18,332	−15,042	−4,353	9,518	6,287	4,750
(15)	Medicare reliance	5,150	10,704	−20,081	−36,337	−1,168	4,008	−8,669	−24,598
(16)	Medicaid generosity (general)	22,397	20,894	23,926	6,046	1,667	−2,884	−10,171	−10,870
(17)	Medicaid generosity for LTC	−12,304	−6,916	−8,411	−9,797	2,202	6,679	7,309	9,896
(18)	VERA-10 health status measure	27,006	15,346	81,835	−3,194	49,358	14,298	−44,972	−59,185
	Facility characteristics								
(19)	Rural or urban status	−5,255	1,286	1,878	−251	1,205	445	−240	4,334
(20)	Residents per full-time MD	−92	−642	335	−4,648	−77	−5,044	855	−12,362
(21)	VA labor index	15,370	−5,956	39,486	−2,484	11,883	−12,594	−14,669	−50,955
(22)	Average food cost per bed day	311	−7,251	−4,232	−844	−346	−1,674	−1,151	−415
(23)	Energy price ($/million Btus)	−5,886	−3,183	−3,569	−75	−4,618	−2,421	2,168	−10,304
(24)	Contract labor cost share	−92	704	426	−235	−185	393	−22	178
(25)	Square feet of building space per acre of land	−2,484	−1,475	26	−1,070	−1,192	−1,271	8,043	366
(26)	Square feet of building space per unique patient	10,616	25,906	31,973	−12,183	6,759	−3,203	−5,350	−63,194

Table C.7—continued

	VISN 1	VISN 2	VISN 3	VISN 4	VISN 5	VISN 6	VISN 7	VISN 8
(27) Research costs per 1,000 unique patients	16,545	-10,645	373	-11,064	4,456	-13,324	-4,043	-23,149
(28) Percentage of funded research	4,211	-1,985	-1,798	-2,960	3,765	-3,731	-957	-7,722
(29) Average building age	-13,535	-9,866	-3,036	-8,724	-3,909	-4,949	-2,123	48,452
(30) Average building condition	1,193	187	5	-24	136	-49	-383	-866
(31) Leased square feet per patient	5,040	-7,580	-3,817	-9,175	-3,984	-8,497	3,310	23,238
(32) Ratio of historic to total number of buildings	-490	5,011	1,382	-2,930	-1,891	1,099	719	-5,891
(33) Total number of buildings	-218	-5,249	-23	1,776	-2,512	1,381	2,211	3,115
(34) Consolidation indicator	1,312	3,029	2,646	-640	692	-1,936	-1,191	-568
(35) Occupancy rate	-88	-6,734	-2,159	443	-53	215	1,730	466
(36) Number of CBOCs per 1,000 unique patients	8,232	23,200	7,079	4,100	993	-7,970	-10,150	-10,740
(37) Direct patient care FTEs per 1,000 unique patients	16,733	-42,520	25,529	-21,779	23,130	732	-13,061	-8,812
(38) Non-patient care FTEs per 1,000 unique patients	-5,075	16,922	-6,891	5,811	-8,548	-1,614	-5,335	10,964
(39) LTC beds per 1,000 unique patients	311	2,241	-1,660	-2,708	-2,280	-789	1,216	3,965
(40) Special program beds per 1,000 unique patients	-1,882	1,961	-1,990	3,946	1,822	-5,178	-1,349	-1,033
Sum of differences—rows (4) through (40)	98,648	8,294	133,695	-128,287	66,690	-29,229	-83,881	-227,880

Table C.7—continued

	VISN 9	VISN 10	VISN 11	VISN 12	VISN 15	VISN 16	VISN 17	VISN 18
(1) Simulated allocations from AVM with VERA-10	970,072	756,284	846,787	1,009,520	696,657	1,713,279	937,036	784,063
(2) Unadjusted average allocation	987,411	722,443	850,068	838,993	771,419	1,841,652	961,778	902,576
(3) Difference (1)–(2)	−17,338	33,841	−3,280	170,526	−74,762	−128,374	−24,742	−118,512
Patient characteristics								
(4) Age	402	−1,481	−758	−1,517	2,558	3,800	−2,611	1,522
(5) Income	285	−382	564	−247	−403	−359	63	−804
(6) Race	9,956	5,175	6,475	2,601	7,823	7,291	−11,034	−10,875
(7) Gender	−632	−412	−522	−469	−642	−232	1,129	626
(8) Martial status	−3,590	2,299	2,629	4,074	−1,378	−5,408	−3,421	−2,142
(9) Physicians per capita	−6,606	−1,656	−817	1,955	−5,493	−3,481	−703	724
(10) Hospital beds per capita	2,580	−2,428	−1,925	−1,069	3,532	6,299	−599	−3,340
(11) Rural or urban status	−5,314	1,440	−353	703	−5,068	−4,142	760	−514
(12) Distance to closest facility	643	−3,461	233	−2,290	300	4,510	3,190	3,590
(13) Distance to closest CBOC	4,644	−10,474	3,216	−9,353	228	45,771	−3,538	11,590
(14) Priority status	4,306	−6,406	−10,220	−539	−4,908	17,783	9,936	−1,136
(15) Medicare reliance	17,939	−10,598	−1,821	15,673	12,307	−6,097	−6,578	19,478
(16) Medicaid generosity (general)	−3,083	6,804	1,471	3,683	2,234	−18,587	−12,304	−12,061
(17) Medicaid generosity for LTC	−485	−13,009	−2,872	−4,139	−1,629	15,469	7,853	11,051
(18) VERA-10 health status measure	−28,466	51,957	−759	93,831	−21,845	−115,126	−8,790	−58,571
Facility characteristics								
(19) Rural or urban status	2,256	−1,009	−5,055	−1,990	−4,013	33	2,243	3,909
(20) Residents per full-time MD	5,167	−1,798	−3,043	4,776	9,046	−3,777	703	−2,099
(21) VA labor index	−15,262	1,523	1,646	15,183	−11,927	−18,626	−20,708	−22,540
(22) Average food cost per bed day	5,489	−3,106	2,778	709	4,121	−3,208	−5,187	−6,152
(23) Energy price ($/million Btus)	2,352	547	2,945	1,054	116	13,320	8,750	−2,572
(24) Contract labor cost share	301	−264	−16	233	−191	−204	313	−127
(25) Square feet of building space per acre of land	−1,903	−759	1,827	2,673	−2,146	10,082	−2,155	−2,102
(26) Square feet of building space per unique patient	5,391	5,788	10,191	25,039	−1,382	−20,596	2,826	−29,619

Table C.7—continued

	VISN 9	VISN 10	VISN 11	VISN 12	VISN 15	VISN 16	VISN 17	VISN 18
(27) Research costs per 1,000 unique patients	-7,849	-3,281	-798	729	-14,925	-13,089	3,718	-8,675
(28) Percentage of funded research	-2,627	955	-1,946	1,249	-3,704	-4,897	733	-3,531
(29) Average building age	-3,166	-5,152	-5,448	-12,506	-454	-6,268	2,689	3,703
(30) Average building condition	-175	10	102	43	-23	272	154	-293
(31) Leased square feet per patient	-8,197	13,998	-2,241	-2,552	-10,148	-4,620	4,500	-3,008
(32) Ratio of historic to total number of buildings	2,472	1,560	3,375	-225	-241	-1,009	2,814	706
(33) Total number of buildings	942	87	490	344	-1,676	2,366	-1,001	1,311
(34) Consolidation indicator	-1,925	-1,361	-875	-3	-841	-3,538	5,195	-1,747
(35) Occupancy rate	73	1,501	1,242	552	2,565	-298	617	2,203
(36) Number of CBOCs per 1,000 unique patients	-3,844	-188	-2,791	819	-4,020	-16,643	2,493	2,356
(37) Direct patient care FTEs per 1,000 unique patients	15,699	16,575	-862	49,015	-35,016	-14,290	9,635	-21,172
(38) Non-patient care FTEs per 1,000 unique patients	-6,424	-6,461	-2,563	-10,552	8,841	1,014	-10,904	9,038
(39) LTC beds per 1,000 unique patients	1,316	-2,916	308	-3,074	1,893	4,029	-4,229	2,439
(40) Special program beds per 1,000 unique patients	-4	225	2,912	-3,889	1,747	4,083	-1,293	322
Sum of differences—rows (4) through (40)	-17,338	33,841	-3,280	170,526	-74,762	-128,373	-24,742	-118,512

Table C.7—continued

	VISN 19	VISN 20	VISN 21	VISN 22	VISN 23
(1) Simulated allocations from AVM with VERA-10	537,276	944,290	1,071,066	1,215,905	970,685
(2) Unadjusted average allocation	557,628	900,785	932,915	1,103,463	919,837
(3) Difference (1)–(2)	–20,352	43,505	138,151	112,441	50,848
Patient characteristics					
(4) Age	–1,042	–4,139	1,860	–3,789	733
(5) Income	–56	20	524	1,812	–380
(6) Race	1,947	6,474	–16,600	–10,117	12,382
(7) Gender	517	1,333	479	421	–578
(8) Martial status	–623	909	4,571	10,790	–2,110
(9) Physicians per capita	–220	–2,457	3,608	7,330	–5,360
(10) Hospital beds per capita	–1,183	–4,705	–5,005	–6,536	4,555
(11) Rural or urban status	–3,003	–1,529	2,767	7,200	–6,850
(12) Distance to closest facility	4,542	–311	3,220	–1,406	8,067
(13) Distance to closest CBOC	698	7,801	–648	–19,301	15,916
(14) Priority status	1,196	20,927	1,317	–9,599	–4,367
(15) Medicare reliance	9,586	12,272	7,347	–30,108	31,593
(16) Medicaid generosity (general)	–2,675	–10,941	–9,310	–11,929	15,693
(17) Medicaid generosity for LTC	–2,803	–1,493	4,623	7,416	–8,641
(18) VERA-10 health status measure	–24,542	2,233	4,444	16,248	8,893
Facility characteristics					
(19) Rural or urban status	–1,124	–2,750	2,035	2,439	–377
(20) Residents per full-time MD	–262	–7,355	–2,428	9,598	13,147
(21) VA labor index	–2,728	4,247	66,938	26,803	–4,629
(22) Average food cost per bed day	770	2,921	8,303	13,209	–5,045
(23) Energy price ($/million Btus)	2,008	3,745	–3,836	–3,428	2,886
(24) Contract labor cost share	–345	–56	–534	–477	199
(25) Square feet of building space per acre of land	–366	–2,817	133	–565	–2,845
(26) Square feet of building space per unique patient	–3,954	3,637	–8,228	2,335	17,249

Table C.7—continued

	VISN 19	VISN 20	VISN 21	VISN 22	VISN 23
(27) Research costs per 1,000 unique patients	-2,061	14,388	39,387	40,623	-7,318
(28) Percentage of funded research	-1,285	4,038	8,784	14,260	-854
(29) Average building age	-7,128	-8,155	17,179	29,540	-7,144
(30) Average building condition	57	205	34	-399	-184
(31) Leased square feet per patient	5,116	4,456	5,756	9,156	-10,750
(32) Ratio of historic to total number of buildings	428	265	-3,505	-3,501	-150
(33) Total number of buildings	409	-603	357	-1,205	-2,303
(34) Consolidation indicator	-358	447	-303	441	1,525
(35) Occupancy rate	-771	732	416	1,130	-3,781
(36) Number of CBOCs per 1,000 unique patients	7,620	-5,806	-415	-2,712	8,389
(37) Direct patient care FTEs per 1,000 unique patients	-7,061	15,816	2,585	23,656	-34,531
(38) Non-patient Care FTEs per 1,000 unique patients	4,356	-6,083	3,126	-2,691	13,071
(39) LTC beds per 1,000 unique patients	2,036	-3,501	-250	166	1,489
(40) Special program beds per 1,000 unique patients	1,955	-663	-579	-4,369	3,256
Sum of differences—rows (4) through (40)	-20,352	43,504	138,151	112,441	50,847

NOTE: Figures shown are in thousands of dollars.

Table C.8
Disaggregation of Simulated Allocations from the All Variables Model with VA DCGs, Excluding Basic Care Priority 7s

	VISN 1	VISN 2	VISN 3	VISN 4	VISN 5	VISN 6	VISN 7	VISN 8
(1) Simulated allocations from AVM with VA DCGs	1,032,708	573,868	1,065,623	944,784	599,771	966,171	1,162,053	1,648,410
(2) Unadjusted average allocation	947,153	567,019	917,287	1,131,336	544,274	1,021,624	1,231,463	1,874,403
(3) Difference (1)–(2)	85,556	6,849	148,335	–186,553	55,496	–55,454	–69,410	–225,993
Patient characteristics								
(4) Age	–2,583	–2,809	–4,676	–2,815	–863	1,604	2,683	–1,123
(5) Income	605	868	1,669	1,239	647	–58	–325	–1,699
(6) Race	6,895	4,287	–2,958	6,585	–569	2,410	1,265	–22,223
(7) Gender	–708	–287	–1,656	–1,390	689	1,251	1,401	–385
(8) Martial status	329	69	1,068	–412	776	–831	–673	–1,983
(9) Physicians per capita	402	–912	2,790	–222	942	–1,583	–1,200	1,420
(10) Hospital beds per capita	–1,279	1,978	2,967	3,242	–374	–1,214	213	5,294
(11) Rural or urban status	778	531	4,230	1,490	1,437	–1,112	–915	5,640
(12) Distance to closest facility	–5,606	3,900	–9,698	–8,479	–4,746	–2,592	1,121	90
(13) Distance to closest CBOC	–6,243	–4,920	–10,525	–7,404	–5,278	12,408	7,768	–10,552
(14) Priority status	6,661	–6,233	–10,462	–9,555	–3,052	7,030	4,511	2,474
(15) Medicare reliance	1,237	4,753	–13,919	–22,791	760	1,425	–6,440	–15,334
(16) Medicaid generosity (general)	32,696	30,501	34,928	8,826	2,434	–4,211	–14,848	–15,868
(17) Medicaid generosity for LTC	–13,875	–7,798	–9,485	–11,048	2,483	7,531	8,242	11,160
(18) VA DCGs health status measure	–5,607	12,147	77,930	–92,532	25,293	–13,494	–53,341	–70,318
Facility characteristics								
(19) Rural or urban status	–4,021	1,069	1,554	–1,080	996	–213	–1,140	3,584
(20) Residents per full-time MD	40	277	–144	2,005	33	2,176	–369	5,334
(21) VA labor index	17,481	–6,774	44,909	–2,825	13,516	–14,324	–16,684	–57,954
(22) Average food cost per bed day	201	–4,683	–2,733	–545	–224	–1,081	–743	–268
(23) Energy price ($/million Btus)	3,522	1,905	2,135	45	2,763	1,448	–1,297	6,165
(24) Contract labor cost share	607	–4,658	–2,820	1,556	1,227	–2,601	146	–1,175
(25) Square feet of building space per acre of land	–5,828	–3,460	61	–2,510	–2,797	–2,981	18,871	859
(26) Square feet of building space per unique patient	10,970	26,770	33,039	–12,590	6,985	–3,309	–5,528	–65,301

Table C.8—continued

	VISN 1	VISN 2	VISN 3	VISN 4	VISN 5	VISN 6	VISN 7	VISN 8
(27) Research costs per 1,000 unique patients	8,793	-5,657	198	-5,880	2,368	-7,081	-2,149	-12,303
(28) Percentage of funded research	17,534	-8,266	-7,487	-12,324	15,677	-15,536	-3,984	-32,150
(29) Average building age	-8,826	-6,433	-1,980	-5,689	-2,549	-3,227	-1,384	31,595
(30) Average building condition	9,997	1,568	41	-205	1,136	-409	-3,213	-7,260
(31) Leased square feet per patient	4,511	-6,785	-3,417	-8,212	-3,566	-7,605	2,963	20,799
(32) Ratio of historic to total number of buildings	-528	5,400	1,489	-3,158	-2,037	1,185	775	-6,349
(33) Total number of buildings	-964	-23,219	-101	7,856	-11,111	6,107	9,781	13,777
(34) Consolidation indicator	5,413	12,496	10,918	-2,641	2,855	-7,986	-4,913	-2,344
(35) Occupancy rate	-160	-12,225	-3,920	805	-95	391	3,140	845
(36) Number of CBOCs per 1,000 unique patients	6,723	18,948	5,782	3,349	811	-6,510	-8,290	-8,772
(37) Direct patient care FTEs per 1,000 unique patients	6,807	-17,297	10,385	-8,860	9,409	298	-5,313	-3,585
(38) Non-patient care FTEs per 1,000 unique patients	189	-630	257	-216	318	60	199	-408
(39) LTC beds per 1,000 unique patients	218	1,569	-1,162	-1,896	-1,597	-553	852	2,776
(40) Special program beds per 1,000 unique patients	-824	859	-871	1,727	798	-2,266	-590	-452
Sum of differences—rows (4) through (40)	85,555	6,849	148,335	-186,552	55,496	-55,453	-69,410	-225,992

Table C.8—continued

	VISN 9	VISN 10	VISN 11	VISN 12	VISN 15	VISN 16	VISN 17	VISN 18
(1) Simulated allocations from AVM with VA DCGs	974,684	755,660	827,256	1,014,321	728,431	1,671,058	929,583	802,436
(2) Unadjusted average allocation	987,411	722,443	850,068	838,993	771,419	1,841,652	961,778	902,576
(3) Difference (1)–(2)	–12,726	33,218	–22,811	175,328	–42,988	–170,594	–32,195	–100,140
Patient characteristics								
(4) Age	2,006	–799	–636	–2,759	798	5,796	1,425	1,104
(5) Income	–582	–576	–122	278	–422	–1,601	–578	–135
(6) Race	6,570	3,478	4,299	1,795	5,113	4,718	–6,466	–7,308
(7) Gender	–674	–439	–556	–500	–684	–248	1,203	667
(8) Marital status	–900	577	659	1,022	–346	–1,357	–858	–537
(9) Physicians per capita	–2,489	–1,209	283	–1,148	–710	–943	324	106
(10) Hospital beds per capita	2,128	–1,239	–698	1,244	2,131	4,972	–529	–4,127
(11) Rural or urban status	–4,668	1,276	–167	474	–4,438	–3,280	639	–248
(12) Distance to closest facility	803	–4,322	291	–2,860	375	5,632	3,984	4,483
(13) Distance to closest CBOC	2,468	–5,568	1,709	–4,972	121	24,331	–1,881	6,161
(14) Priority status	2,137	–5,525	–7,398	–2,194	–4,524	8,984	7,654	468
(15) Medicare reliance	8,515	–6,059	–3,468	8,409	4,965	–3,324	–551	13,345
(16) Medicaid generosity (general)	–4,500	9,932	2,147	5,377	3,261	–27,133	–17,962	–17,608
(17) Medicaid generosity for LTC	–547	–14,670	–3,238	–4,667	–1,837	17,444	8,855	12,462
(18) VA DCGs health status measure	16,014	36,107	–17,912	116,244	31,816	–123,565	–28,785	–29,678
Facility characteristics								
(19) Rural or urban status	1,878	590	–6,321	–974	–3,349	–1,267	1,886	6,444
(20) Residents per full-time MD	–2,229	776	1,313	–2,061	–3,903	1,630	–303	906
(21) VA labor index	–17,358	1,732	1,872	17,269	–13,565	–21,184	–23,553	–25,636
(22) Average food cost per bed day	3,545	–2,006	1,794	458	2,662	–2,072	–3,350	–3,974
(23) Energy price ($/million Btus)	–1,407	–327	–1,762	–631	–70	–7,970	–5,236	1,539
(24) Contract labor cost share	–1,989	1,744	107	–1,545	1,263	1,352	–2,073	837
(25) Square feet of building space per acre of land	–4,466	–1,781	4,287	6,272	–5,035	23,656	–5,057	–4,932
(26) Square feet of building space per unique patient	5,571	5,981	10,531	25,873	–1,428	–21,282	2,920	–30,606

Table C.8—continued

	VISN 9	VISN 10	VISN 11	VISN 12	VISN 15	VISN 16	VISN 17	VISN 18
(27) Research costs per 1,000 unique patients	-4,171	-1,744	-424	388	-7,932	-6,956	1,976	-4,610
(28) Percentage of funded research	-10,938	3,976	-8,101	5,201	-15,422	-20,388	3,053	-14,703
(29) Average building age	-2,065	-3,359	-3,553	-8,155	-296	-4,088	1,754	2,415
(30) Average building condition	-1,470	84	854	358	-194	2,281	1,294	-2,459
(31) Leased square feet per patient	-7,337	12,529	-2,006	-2,284	-9,083	-4,135	4,027	-2,693
(32) Ratio of historic to total number of buildings	2,664	1,682	3,637	-242	-259	-1,087	3,032	761
(33) Total number of buildings	4,167	384	2,165	1,523	-7,412	10,466	-4,426	5,799
(34) Consolidation indicator	-7,940	-5,616	-3,610	-13	-3,471	-14,598	21,431	-7,206
(35) Occupancy rate	132	2,725	2,254	1,002	4,656	-541	1,120	3,999
(36) Number of CBOCs per 1,000 unique patients	-3,139	-154	-2,279	669	-3,283	-13,593	2,036	1,924
(37) Direct patient care FTEs per 1,000 unique patients	6,386	6,743	-351	19,939	-14,244	-5,813	3,919	-8,613
(38) Non-patient care FTEs per 1,000 unique patients	239	241	95	393	-329	-38	406	-337
(39) LTC beds per 1,000 unique patients	921	-2,042	215	-2,152	1,325	2,821	-2,961	1,707
(40) Special program beds per 1,000 unique patients	-2	99	1,275	-1,702	765	1,787	-566	141
Sum of differences—rows (4) through (40)	-12,726	33,218	-22,811	175,327	-42,987	-170,594	-32,195	-100,139

Table C.8—continued

	VISN 19	VISN 20	VISN 21	VISN 22	VISN 23
(1) Simulated allocations from AVM with VA DCGs	589,931	976,334	1,078,942	1,186,340	997,165
(2) Unadjusted average allocation	557,628	900,785	932,915	1,103,463	919,837
(3) Difference (1)–(2)	32,303	75,549	146,028	82,876	77,327
Patient characteristics					
(4) Age	286	1,841	1,602	2,783	-2,862
(5) Income	442	-533	597	134	153
(6) Race	1,235	3,425	-13,290	-6,739	7,477
(7) Gender	551	1,421	510	449	-616
(8) Martial status	-156	228	1,147	2,707	-529
(9) Physicians per capita	312	-402	1,028	4,156	-944
(10) Hospital beds per capita	-1,941	-4,655	-5,721	-6,397	4,005
(11) Rural or urban status	-2,696	-1,034	2,365	5,543	-5,846
(12) Distance to closest facility	5,672	-389	4,021	-1,755	10,074
(13) Distance to closest CBOC	371	4,147	-344	-10,260	8,461
(14) Priority status	1,391	14,739	1,715	-6,672	-2,148
(15) Medicare reliance	5,805	10,759	7,648	-10,444	14,708
(16) Medicaid generosity (general)	-3,904	-15,972	-13,591	-17,414	22,909
(17) Medicaid generosity for LTC	-3,161	-1,684	5,213	8,363	-9,744
(18) VA DCGs health status measure	34,124	37,424	-349	-30,315	78,798
Facility characteristics					
(19) Rural or urban status	1,500	-3,751	1,678	2,013	-1,078
(20) Residents per full-time MD	113	3,173	1,048	-4,141	-5,672
(21) VA labor index	-3,103	4,830	76,132	30,484	-5,265
(22) Average food cost per bed day	497	1,886	5,362	8,531	-3,258
(23) Energy price ($/million Btus)	-1,201	-2,241	2,295	2,051	-1,727
(24) Contract labor cost share	2,281	370	3,531	3,157	-1,318
(25) Square feet of building space per acre of land	-860	-6,609	311	-1,326	-6,676
(26) Square feet of building space per unique patient	-4,086	3,758	-8,502	2,413	17,824

Table C.8—continued

	VISN 19	VISN 20	VISN 21	VISN 22	VISN 23
(27) Research costs per 1,000 unique patients	−1,095	7,647	20,932	21,590	−3,889
(28) Percentage of funded research	−5,352	16,812	36,576	59,376	−3,555
(29) Average building age	−4,648	−5,318	11,203	19,263	−4,658
(30) Average building condition	481	1,718	284	−3,347	−1,539
(31) Leased square feet per patient	4,579	3,988	5,152	8,195	−9,622
(32) Ratio of historic to total number of buildings	461	286	−3,778	−3,772	−161
(33) Total number of buildings	1,810	−2,666	1,579	−5,329	−10,188
(34) Consolidation indicator	−1,479	1,843	−1,250	1,819	6,293
(35) Occupancy rate	−1,400	1,328	755	2,051	−6,864
(36) Number of CBOCs per 1,000 unique patients	6,223	−4,742	−339	−2,215	6,851
(37) Direct patient care FTEs per 1,000 unique patients	−2,872	6,434	1,051	9,623	−14,047
(38) Non-patient care FTEs per 1,000 unique patients	−162	227	−116	100	−487
(39) LTC beds per 1,000 unique patients	1,426	−2,451	−175	116	1,043
(40) Special program beds per 1,000 unique patients	856	−290	−253	−1,913	1,425
Sum of differences—rows (4) through (40)	32,303	75,548	146,026	82,875	77,327

NOTE: Figures shown are in thousands of dollars.

Table C.9
Regression Results for the All Variables Regression Models, Including Basic Care Priority 7s

Variable Category		Base Regression Model (VERA-10) 0.46[a]		Selected Variables Regression Model (VERA-10) 0.49[a]		Selected Variables Regression Model with VA DCGs 0.62[a]	
		Estimate	t-Statistic	Estimate	t-Statistic	Estimate	t-Statistic
Intercept		-2116.13	-1.95	-4873.98	-4.72 **	-3340.77	-2.84 **
Patient characteristics							
Age	Less than 25			Reference		Reference	
	25–34			390.21	7.30 **	388.72	8.47 **
	35–44			804.71	13.12 **	661.97	11.53 **
	45–54			1320.17	20.24 **	974.32	16.55 **
	55–64			1799.08	26.60 **	1175.46	19.34 **
	65–74			1183.12	16.80 **	735.93	11.63 **
	75–84			1212.77	16.39 **	560.80	8.38 **
	85 and over			1070.67	12.49 **	159.22	2.09 *
Income	Missing			-29.43	-0.98	-270.94	-10.25 **
	$20,000 or less			341.71	9.59 **	136.78	4.77 **
	$21,000–$40,000			475.94	11.79 **	353.56	11.97 **
	$41,000–$60,000			71.63	3.30 **	95.77	5.36 **
	$61,000–$80,000			96.16	3.04 **	107.16	3.54 **
	More than $80,000			Reference		Reference	
Race/ethnicity	Hispanic			-669.41	-3.89 **	-381.02	-2.88 **
	American Indian			-345.83	-2.00 *	-422.72	-2.56 *
	Black			-68.79	-0.96	25.82	0.42
	Asian			-1052.71	-4.20 **	-758.21	-1.99 *
	White			Reference		Reference	
Gender	Female			-101.07	-2.71 **	-282.85	-9.90 **
	Male			Reference		Reference	
Marital status	Single			442.02	22.60 **	201.04	11.00 **
	Married			Reference		Reference	
Physicians per capita	Less than 0.001			-123.86	-2.02 *	55.01	1.07
	0.001 to 0.002			-88.36	-1.54	54.88	1.04
	0.0021 to 0.003			68.35	1.18	101.25	2.03 *
	Greater than 0.003			Reference		Reference	

Table C.9—continued

Variable Category		Base Regression Model (VERA-10) 0.46[a]		Selected Variables Regression Model (VERA-10) 0.49[a]		Selected Variables Regression Model with VA DCGs 0.62[a]	
		Estimate	t-Statistic	Estimate	t-Statistic	Estimate	t-Statistic
Hospital beds per capita	Less than 0.003			-198.10	-3.38 **	-114.87	-1.95
	0.003 to 0.006			-148.63	-2.70 **	-41.79	-0.76
	Greater than 0.006			Reference		Reference	
Rural or urban status	Urban			82.54	1.36	84.71	1.72
	Suburban			-12.90	-0.27	10.17	0.25
	Rural			-57.13	-1.50	-64.49	-1.82
	Very rural			Reference		Reference	
Distance to closest facility				1.65	2.15 *	2.53	3.91 **
Distance to closest CBOC				6.37	6.22 **	2.87	2.66 **
Priority Group	1			1584.02	30.11 **	443.84	11.70 **
	2			835.52	24.37 **	311.94	10.26 **
	3			586.01	16.84 **	155.84	5.25 **
	4			3418.66	34.64 **	1551.98	16.27 **
	5			668.55	20.48 **	22.75	0.83
	6			9.85	0.32	-121.26	-4.74 **
	7			Reference		Reference	
Medicare reliance	Not eligible			Reference		Reference	
	No reliance			2114.75	33.30 **	1251.16	28.44 **
	FFS—1 to 24%			3509.57	36.70 **	1945.05	33.27 **
	FFS—25 to 49%			689.54	15.88 **	149.20	4.44 **
	FFS—50 to 74%			-114.90	-2.57 *	-353.50	-8.56 **
	FFS—75 to 100%			-1023.60	-16.81 **	-811.77	-19.43 **
	HMO—1 to 24%			23900.19	34.52 **	17624.81	23.00 **
	HMO—25 to 49%			6981.64	20.11 **	3379.31	11.55 **
	HMO—50 to 74%			1233.05	13.45 **	394.68	4.41 **
	HMO—75 to 100%			-960.93	-12.59 **	-520.84	-9.06 **

Table C.9—continued

Variable Category	Base Regression Model (VERA-10) 0.46[a]		Selected Variables Regression Model (VERA-10) 0.49[a]		Selected Variables Regression Model with VA DCGs 0.62[a]	
	Estimate	t–Statistic	Estimate	t–Statistic	Estimate	t–Statistic
Medicaid generosity (general)			0.02	0.68	0.04	1.17
Medicaid generosity for LTC			−0.003	−0.22	−0.004	−0.27
VERA-10 patient category						
1 Non-Reliant	Reference		Reference			
2 Basic Medical	1,828.61	30.71 **	1,520.60	17.94 **		
3 Mental Health	3,231.00	47.20 ***	2,336.87	26.32 **		
4 Heart, Lung, and GI	2,731.87	29.18 ***	2,327.46	26.08 **		
5 Oncology	6,351.01	41.09 **	5,435.91	40.25 **		
6 Multiple Problem	15,455.32	59.12 **	13,424.41	59.52 **		
7 Specialized Care	15,958.43	52.50 **	13,833.65	50.97 **		
8 Supportive Care	22,608.68	52.69 **	19,588.63	48.96 **		
9 Chronic Mental Illness	29,738.11	49.74 **	26,772.18	45.78 **		
10 Critically Ill	53,479.27	111.75 **	49,311.08	114.78 **		
VA DCG patient category						
DCG 0.1					Reference	
DCG 0.2					363.89	19.81 **
DCG 0.3					665.03	27.57 **
DCG 0.4					476.90	19.36 **
DCG 0.5					796.02	28.46 **
DCG 0.7					885.84	31.99 **
DCG 1					1,365.38	35.69 **
DCG 1.5					1,851.96	39.07 **
DCG 2					2,253.88	38.25 **
DCG 2.5					2,502.24	40.01 **
DCG 3					3,334.45	39.82 **
DCG 4					4,297.35	38.26 **
DCG 5					5,565.02	42.31 **
DCG 6					7,936.01	47.71 **
DCG 7.5					12,296.07	52.60 **

Table C.9—continued

Variable Category		Base Regression Model (VERA-10) 0.46[a]		Selected Variables Regression Model (VERA-10) 0.49[a]		Selected Variables Regression Model with VA DCGs 0.62[a]	
		Estimate	t-Statistic	Estimate	t-Statistic	Estimate	t-Statistic
DCG 10						22,520.40	66.55 **
DCG 15						34,718.47	74.00 **
DCG 20						41,547.21	83.26 **
DCG 25						47,442.92	96.74 **
DCG 30						53,399.35	113.76 **
DCG 40						59,875.14	147.17 **
DCG 50						61,949.63	120.15 **
DCG 60						64,197.96	136.61 **
DCG 70						64,551.43	101.68 **
Facility characteristics							
Rural or urban status of facility	Urban			−297.16	−1.36	−472.19	−2.57 *
	Suburban			−457.95	−2.08 *	−679.33	−3.71 **
	Rural			−498.83	−2.04 *	−541.94	−2.69 **
	Very rural			Reference		Reference	
Residents per full-time MD		352.70	3.70 **	128.61	2.39 *	−93.83	−1.15
VA labor index		19.62	1.81	22.73	2.20 *	26.49	2.17 *
Average food cost per bed day				18.62	1.40	11.62	0.74
Energy price (dollars per million Btus)				−11.32	−0.48	19.78	0.74
Contract labor costs				−7.82	−0.63	1.64	0.11
Square feet of building space per acre of land				1.73	1.19	3.49	3.69 **
Square feet of building space per unique patient				11.36	2.84 **	11.59	2.48 *
Research costs per unique patient		3.66	6.41 **	1.64	2.37 *	0.58	0.78
Percentage of funded research				5533.80	1.06	18318.59	3.38 **
Average building age as of 2001				−7.26	−2.52 *	−4.69	−1.35
Average building condition (scale of 1–5)				−11.01	−0.22	−57.94	−1.00
Leased square feet per patient				75.63	1.44	67.50	1.24
Ratio of historic to total number of buildings				124.82	0.81	163.25	0.90
Total number of buildings				−0.64	−0.52	−2.11	−1.56
Indicator for recent facility/management consolidation				11.37	0.15	130.98	1.37
Occupancy rate				−119.06	−0.72	−175.63	−0.86

Table C.9—continued

Variable Category	Base Regression Model (VERA-10) 0.46[a]		Selected Variables Regression Model (VERA-10) 0.49[a]		Selected Variables Regression Model with VA DCGs 0.62[a]	
	Estimate	t-Statistic	Estimate	t-Statistic	Estimate	t-Statistic
Number of CBOCs per 1,000 unique patients			554.83	2.23 *	334.42	0.93
Direct patient care FTEs per 1,000 unique patients			74.57	2.75 **	20.38	0.65
Non-patient care FTEs per 1,000 unique patients			–7.15	–0.85	0.82	0.07
LTC beds per 1,000 unique patients			–9.01	–1.12	–6.05	–0.38
Special program beds per 1,000 unique patients			–85.89	–1.79	–47.02	–0.95

NOTES: * indicates significance at the 95% level and ** at the 99% level. Robust t-statistics are calculated by clustering data at the facility level.
[a]R-squared.

Table C.10
Comparison of Actual and Simulated Allocations from the All Variables Models, Including Basic Care Priority 7s

VISN	VERA FY 03 Actual Allocation	Base Regression Model		Selected Variables Model with VERA-10		Selected Variables Model with VA DCGs	
		Simulated Allocation	% diff FY 03	Simulated Allocation	% diff FY 03	Simulated Allocation	% diff FY 03
01 Boston	1,012,354	1,056,309	4.3%	1,050,807	3.8%	1,036,127	2.3%
02 Albany	556,418	575,758	3.5%	578,229	3.9%	576,448	3.6%
03 Bronx	1,111,597	1,111,420	0.0%	1,078,656	−3.0%	1,095,092	−1.5%
04 Pittsburgh	1,076,519	1,119,119	4.0%	1,013,609	−5.8%	948,478	−11.9%
05 Baltimore	617,523	594,717	−3.7%	592,150	−4.1%	581,568	−5.8%
06 Durham	990,671	960,553	−3.0%	985,169	−0.6%	960,060	−3.1%
07 Atlanta	1,158,656	1,130,577	−2.4%	1,141,822	−1.5%	1,163,053	0.4%
08 Bay Pines	1,655,761	1,720,476	3.9%	1,658,762	0.2%	1,656,767	0.1%
09 Nashville	926,758	931,436	0.5%	968,909	4.5%	966,519	4.3%
10 Cincinnati	771,274	748,949	−2.9%	753,432	−2.3%	753,775	−2.3%
11 Ann Arbor	849,127	850,405	0.2%	860,101	1.3%	840,181	−1.1%
12 Chicago	978,050	981,358	0.3%	1,014,596	3.7%	1,020,783	4.4%
15 Kansas City	761,453	738,673	−3.0%	706,052	−7.3%	736,654	−3.3%
16 Jackson	1,688,502	1,598,637	−5.3%	1,687,346	−0.1%	1,645,028	−2.6%
17 Dallas	936,733	909,684	−2.9%	914,879	−2.3%	907,288	−3.1%
18 Phoenix	803,265	821,635	2.3%	809,491	0.8%	830,773	3.4%
19 Denver	528,463	520,636	−1.5%	535,616	1.4%	591,354	11.9%
20 Portland	902,764	872,276	−3.4%	909,734	0.8%	944,627	4.6%
21 San Francisco	1,062,177	1,066,032	0.4%	1,071,513	0.9%	1,075,937	1.3%
22 Long Beach	1,219,641	1,210,171	−0.8%	1,194,022	−2.1%	1,167,800	−4.3%
23 Lincoln & Minneapolis	917,822	1,006,707	9.7%	1,000,632	9.0%	1,027,214	11.9%
Total amount redistributed		290,983		265,431		387,115	
% of FY 03 dollars redistributed		1.4%		1.3%		1.9%	

NOTE: Figures shown are in thousands of dollars.

Table C.11
Disaggregation of Simulated Allocations from the All Variables Model with VERA-10, Including Basic Care Priority 7s

	VISN 1	VISN 2	VISN 3	VISN 4	VISN 5	VISN 6	VISN 7	VISN 8
(1) Simulated allocations from AVM with VERA-10	1,050,807	578,229	1,078,656	1,013,609	592,150	985,169	1,141,822	1,658,762
(2) Unadjusted average allocation	982,277	606,669	1,047,663	1,177,746	516,972	979,348	1,181,266	1,896,603
(3) Difference (1)–(2)	68,530	–28,439	30,993	–164,137	75,178	5,821	–39,444	–237,842
Patient characteristics								
(4) Age	1,791	–3,998	–2,234	2,640	–1,388	–1,628	–828	6,208
(5) Income	–1,060	–3,205	–10,456	–2,073	229	5,101	3,135	2,663
(6) Race	7,766	5,700	–2,285	9,734	1,519	5,675	6,048	–35,319
(7) Gender	336	21	440	726	–64	–154	–229	300
(8) Martial status	893	–369	3,823	–3,376	4,282	–3,272	–2,540	–9,802
(9) Physicians per capita	5,845	–1,380	12,258	693	2,656	–6,049	–5,117	5,554
(10) Hospital beds per capita	–2,491	630	1,227	2,656	1,676	171	1,387	3,838
(11) Rural or urban status	560	403	5,723	1,581	1,464	–1,218	–1,532	6,737
(12) Distance to closest facility	–5,514	4,216	–10,172	–8,032	–3,973	–2,725	818	–10
(13) Distance to closest CBOC	–12,685	–10,514	–23,895	–15,540	–9,665	23,968	15,247	–22,950
(14) Priority status	–4,133	–9,890	–34,882	–30,375	–1,248	15,410	11,512	–10,213
(15) Medicare reliance	4,491	8,009	–34,866	–36,550	567	7,090	–4,967	–32,135
(16) Medicaid generosity (general)	11,521	11,064	13,573	2,789	639	–1,710	–5,195	–6,305
(17) Medicaid generosity for LTC	–3,632	–2,088	–2,741	–2,887	621	1,902	2,074	3,134
(18) VERA-10 health status measure	19,432	20	31,607	–15,390	55,491	25,071	–30,956	–53,155
Facility characteristics								
(19) Rural or urban status	–6,281	1,635	2,597	343	1,346	372	–243	5,195
(20) Residents per full-time MD	–61	–512	–338	–4,385	–221	–3,893	616	–11,657
(21) VA labor index	13,358	–5,662	39,186	–2,582	9,425	–10,566	–12,322	–44,615
(22) Average food cost per bed day	770	–8,479	–5,113	–865	–332	–1,566	–1,024	–651
(23) Energy price ($/million Btus)	–3,648	–1,953	–2,338	8	–2,392	–1,215	1,286	–6,223
(24) Contract labor cost share	–933	5,535	3,173	–1,768	–1,215	2,694	–263	1,856
(25) Square feet of building space per acre of land	–3,298	–2,049	–374	–1,353	–1,493	–1,531	10,872	619
(26) Square feet of building space per unique patient	12,077	31,839	40,212	–14,330	7,318	–4,050	–6,158	–74,995

Table C.11—continued

	VISN 1	VISN 2	VISN 3	VISN 4	VISN 5	VISN 6	VISN 7	VISN 8
(27) Research costs per 1,000 unique patients	17,568	−10,473	−1,186	−10,603	3,757	−11,471	−3,278	−22,063
(28) Percentage of funded research	7,437	−3,308	−3,575	−4,951	5,680	−5,518	−1,258	−12,369
(29) Average building age	−15,127	−11,212	−5,575	−10,014	−4,112	−3,587	−1,341	55,621
(30) Average building condition	2,833	459	75	−24	281	−139	−836	−2,259
(31) Leased square feet per patient	5,593	−8,964	−4,735	−10,313	−4,000	−8,723	3,962	24,552
(32) Ratio of historic to total number of buildings	−527	5,263	2,138	−2,847	−1,836	554	473	−6,011
(33) Total number of buildings	−294	−9,019	−192	2,981	−3,801	2,237	3,504	5,354
(34) Consolidation indicator	467	1,137	1,054	−257	223	−659	−427	−286
(35) Occupancy rate	−75	−12,202	−3,143	923	−58	471	2,894	960
(36) Number of CBOCs per 1,000 unique patients	6,981	20,835	6,833	3,810	760	−6,857	−8,820	−9,841
(37) Direct patient care FTEs per 1,000 unique patients	15,738	−42,767	29,247	−21,011	20,734	2,496	−10,560	−14,867
(38) Non-patient care FTEs per 1,000 unique patients	−4,596	15,998	−7,629	4,513	−7,311	−1,786	−4,849	10,865
(39) LTC beds per 1,000 unique patients	471	3,455	−3,329	−4,613	−3,141	−734	1,620	5,973
(40) Special program beds per 1,000 unique patients	−3,043	3,383	−3,115	6,603	2,761	−8,339	−2,148	−1,542
Sum of differences—rows (4) through (40)	68,530	−28,439	30,992	−164,136	75,178	5,821	−39,444	−237,840

Table C.11—continued

	VISN 9	VISN 10	VISN 11	VISN 12	VISN 15	VISN 16	VISN 17	VISN 18
(1) Simulated allocations from AVM with VERA-10	968,909	753,432	860,101	1,014,596	706,052	1,687,346	914,879	809,491
(2) Unadjusted average allocation	967,279	686,732	867,636	876,677	770,012	1,709,170	904,688	948,652
(3) Difference (1)–(2)	1,631	66,700	-7,535	137,919	-63,960	-21,823	10,191	-139,161
Patient characteristics								
(4) Age	-3,263	-179	150	-2,334	3,786	7,951	-21	-5,866
(5) Income	1,079	3,871	-2,474	-3,249	1,070	10,994	3,958	-2,236
(6) Race	8,699	5,319	6,896	4,446	6,830	9,045	-10,283	-13,905
(7) Gender	-198	216	202	66	476	358	-443	-1,104
(8) Martial status	-3,651	3,355	2,146	3,412	-2,416	-3,895	-2,518	-2,621
(9) Physicians per capita	-8,053	-2,653	-1,292	-680	-5,195	-4,229	-978	1,000
(10) Hospital beds per capita	1,992	-2,176	-1,758	-899	3,472	5,890	-709	-3,011
(11) Rural or urban status	-3,868	1,025	-448	395	-4,717	-3,451	618	-267
(12) Distance to closest facility	171	-3,751	471	-2,080	1,103	4,499	3,369	3,241
(13) Distance to closest CBOC	3,646	-10,206	3,627	-9,506	1,069	46,270	-3,201	17,094
(14) Priority status	16,389	-1,754	-11,902	-2,348	-10,475	26,166	17,442	15,010
(15) Medicare reliance	18,947	-6,279	-933	14,465	14,537	7,335	-3,227	13,661
(16) Medicaid generosity (general)	-1,683	3,018	561	1,757	765	-8,838	-6,014	-6,638
(17) Medicaid generosity for LTC	-80	-3,482	-752	-1,226	-363	4,167	2,165	3,341
(18) VERA-10 health status measure	-20,419	62,706	-6,043	73,664	-12,465	-60,314	10,372	-78,652
Facility characteristics								
(19) Rural or urban status	2,623	-1,394	-6,501	-3,324	-4,354	663	2,482	4,729
(20) Residents per full-time MD	4,735	-1,390	-2,887	3,773	7,567	-2,960	643	-1,098
(21) VA labor index	-13,044	1,025	1,179	13,353	-10,396	-15,207	-16,831	-20,593
(22) Average food cost per bed day	5,133	-3,131	3,234	715	4,345	-3,033	-5,257	-6,862
(23) Energy price ($/million Btus)	1,474	346	1,849	726	140	7,256	4,833	-1,436
(24) Contract labor cost share	2,173	-1,869	-193	1,783	-1,360	-1,421	2,098	-1,553
(25) Square feet of building space per acre of land	-2,319	-826	2,405	3,194	-2,769	12,841	-2,555	-2,948
(26) Square feet of building space per unique patient	3,582	6,220	12,988	31,568	-1,593	-24,008	2,656	-36,851

Table C.11—continued

	VISN 9	VISN 10	VISN 11	VISN 12	VISN 15	VISN 16	VISN 17	VISN 18
(27) Research costs per 1,000 unique patients	-6,780	-2,832	-1,313	968	-13,745	-10,840	3,458	-7,765
(28) Percentage of funded research	-4,229	1,505	-3,258	1,536	-5,957	-6,919	1,234	-5,062
(29) Average building age	-3,154	-5,204	-7,363	-15,279	-634	-4,491	3,226	2,984
(30) Average building condition	-325	25	257	108	-84	581	326	-675
(31) Leased square feet per patient	-7,881	15,357	-2,164	-3,410	-11,346	-4,748	5,336	-2,366
(32) Ratio of historic to total number of buildings	1,941	1,384	3,929	-91	-133	-1,171	2,437	1,139
(33) Total number of buildings	1,658	160	613	440	-2,388	3,704	-1,457	2,150
(34) Consolidation indicator	-671	-459	-283	-100	-280	-1,166	1,698	-657
(35) Occupancy rate	232	2,459	2,312	1,061	4,150	-336	1,072	3,674
(36) Number of CBOCs per 1,000 unique patients	-3,904	-411	-2,587	771	-4,233	-13,561	1,511	2,348
(37) Direct patient care FTEs per 1,000 unique patients	13,367	15,756	-816	46,197	-30,823	-11,192	9,278	-19,669
(38) Non-patient care FTEs per 1,000 unique patients	-4,965	-5,617	-2,527	-9,911	6,882	697	-9,171	8,304
(39) LTC beds per 1,000 unique patients	2,116	-3,780	364	-5,547	2,672	5,512	-5,367	3,745
(40) Special program beds per 1,000 unique patients	160	342	4,774	-6,495	2,899	6,027	-1,989	252
Sum of differences—rows (4) through (40)	1,630	66,700	-7,535	137,919	-63,960	-21,823	10,191	-139,160

Table C.11—continued

	VISN 19	VISN 20	VISN 21	VISN 22	VISN 23
(1) Simulated allocations from AVM with VERA-10	535,616	909,734	1,071,513	1,194,022	1,000,632
(2) Unadjusted average allocation	550,889	829,897	932,075	1,062,980	1,030,298
(3) Difference (1)–(2)	–15,273	79,837	139,438	131,042	–29,666
Patient characteristics					
(4) Age	699	250	1,459	–2,869	–328
(5) Income	340	4,261	–1,132	–2,212	–8,603
(6) Race	533	3,406	–19,523	–10,546	10,244
(7) Gender	–31	–349	–606	–243	278
(8) Martial status	–879	2,632	6,130	15,025	–6,358
(9) Physicians per capita	613	–1,063	4,393	10,100	–6,424
(10) Hospital beds per capita	–1,216	–4,356	–5,292	–6,079	5,045
(11) Rural or urban status	–2,993	–1,553	2,463	6,230	–7,152
(12) Distance to closest facility	5,408	–535	3,710	–1,402	11,187
(13) Distance to closest CBOC	1,291	6,706	–1,293	–19,021	19,559
(14) Priority status	–1,838	24,323	10,577	5,504	–23,273
(15) Medicare reliance	11,693	16,049	4,536	–29,681	27,257
(16) Medicaid generosity (general)	–1,508	–5,341	–4,906	–6,010	8,460
(17) Medicaid generosity for LTC	–710	–270	1,410	2,102	–2,688
(18) VERA-10 health status measure	–19,936	23,241	2,257	21,557	–28,087
Facility characteristics					
(19) Rural or urban status	–1,548	–3,090	2,411	2,772	–435
(20) Residents per full-time MD	–498	–5,797	–2,070	8,083	12,348
(21) VA labor index	–2,472	3,050	56,823	21,624	–4,733
(22) Average food cost per bed day	907	2,924	9,782	14,683	–6,180
(23) Energy price ($/million Btus)	1,273	1,983	–2,113	–1,838	1,982
(24) Contract labor cost share	–2,481	–504	–3,893	–3,480	1,621
(25) Square feet of building space per acre of land	–563	–3,403	288	–503	–4,237
(26) Square feet of building space per unique patient	–4,128	2,634	–9,200	2,038	22,183

Table C.11—continued

	VISN 19	VISN 20	VISN 21	VISN 22	VISN 23
(27) Research costs per 1,000 unique patients	-2,210	11,768	39,364	36,010	-8,334
(28) Percentage of funded research	-2,175	5,722	15,623	21,650	-1,810
(29) Average building age	-7,925	-7,874	18,725	31,064	-8,727
(30) Average building condition	137	438	158	-841	-495
(31) Leased square feet per patient	5,484	4,652	7,170	9,750	-13,207
(32) Ratio of historic to total number of buildings	554	75	-3,628	-3,480	-164
(33) Total number of buildings	686	-790	387	-1,776	-4,156
(34) Consolidation indicator	-121	105	-57	135	602
(35) Occupancy rate	-1,114	1,256	660	1,900	-7,096
(36) Number of CBOCs per 1,000 unique patients	6,533	-4,699	-831	-2,661	8,024
(37) Direct patient care FTEs per 1,000 unique patients	-6,669	13,674	5,949	22,693	-36,756
(38) Non-patient care FTEs per 1,000 unique patients	3,704	-4,738	1,958	-2,546	12,725
(39) LTC beds per 1,000 unique patients	2,790	-4,172	-565	350	2,181
(40) Special program beds per 1,000 unique patients	3,095	-777	-1,686	-7,043	5,879
(41) Sum of differences—rows (4) through (40)	-15,273	79,836	139,437	131,041	-29,666

NOTE: Figures shown are in thousands of dollars.

Table C.12
Disaggregation of Simulated Allocations from the All Variables Model with VA DCGs, Including Basic Care Priority 7s

	VISN 1	VISN 2	VISN 3	VISN 4	VISN 5	VISN 6	VISN 7	VISN 8
(1) Simulated allocations from AVM with VA DCGs	1,036,127	576,448	1,095,092	948,478	581,568	960,060	1,163,053	1,656,767
(2) Unadjusted average allocation	982,277	606,669	1,047,663	1,177,746	516,972	979,348	1,181,266	1,896,603
(3) Difference (1)–(2)	53,850	–30,221	47,429	–229,268	64,597	–19,288	–18,213	–239,836
Patient characteristics								
(4) Age	–3,133	–4,052	–8,001	–4,426	166	3,313	4,863	–3,710
(5) Income	–350	–3,328	–10,045	–522	510	6,446	2,864	3,754
(6) Race	3,170	2,702	–259	5,733	2,802	5,215	7,182	–21,099
(7) Gender	940	59	1,230	2,032	–179	–430	–641	841
(8) Martial status	406	–168	1,739	–1,535	1,947	–1,488	–1,155	–4,458
(9) Physicians per capita	–2,470	–1,982	–422	–246	411	205	–388	3,505
(10) Hospital beds per capita	–976	1,691	3,022	2,313	–999	–867	–106	4,890
(11) Rural or urban status	616	637	5,241	1,673	1,369	–969	–1,043	6,308
(12) Distance to closest facility	–8,448	6,460	–15,584	–12,306	–6,088	–4,174	1,253	–15
(13) Distance to closest CBOC	–5,724	–4,745	–10,782	–7,012	–4,361	10,815	6,880	–10,356
(14) Priority status	1,109	–3,526	–9,361	–10,320	–1,363	5,218	5,147	–3,137
(15) Medicare reliance	2,063	4,132	–22,284	–22,199	1,276	3,401	–4,836	–19,294
(16) Medicaid generosity (general)	25,235	24,234	29,731	6,109	1,400	–3,746	–11,380	–13,810
(17) Medicaid generosity for LTC	–5,239	–3,011	–3,954	–4,164	896	2,743	2,992	4,521
(18) VA DCGs health status measure	–29,088	–17,975	–897	–131,643	36,338	11,727	–23,327	–81,224
Facility characteristics								
(19) Rural or urban status	–4,915	1,635	2,586	–492	1,339	–293	–1,247	5,174
(20) Residents per full-time MD	44	373	247	3,199	161	2,840	–450	8,504
(21) VA labor index	15,569	–6,599	45,674	–3,010	10,986	–12,315	–14,362	–52,003
(22) Average food cost per bed day	481	–5,292	–3,191	–540	–207	–978	–639	–406
(23) Energy price ($/million Btus)	6,373	3,412	4,086	–15	4,179	2,122	–2,247	10,873
(24) Contract labor cost share	196	–1,162	–666	371	255	–566	55	–390
(25) Square feet of building space per acre of land	–6,652	–4,132	–754	–2,729	–3,011	–3,088	21,931	1,249
(26) Square feet of building space per unique patient	12,326	32,495	41,040	–14,625	7,468	–4,134	–6,285	–76,539

Table C.12—continued

	VISN 1	VISN 2	VISN 3	VISN 4	VISN 5	VISN 6	VISN 7	VISN 8
(27) Research costs per 1,000 unique patients	6,261	−3,733	−423	−3,779	1,339	−4,088	−1,168	−7,863
(28) Percentage of funded research	24,618	−10,949	−11,833	−16,390	18,803	−18,266	−4,163	−40,944
(29) Average building age	−9,773	−7,244	−3,602	−6,469	−2,657	−2,318	−866	35,934
(30) Average building condition	14,914	2,416	393	−125	1,477	−731	−4,400	−11,890
(31) Leased square feet per patient	4,992	−8,000	−4,226	−9,204	−3,570	−7,785	3,536	21,913
(32) Ratio of historic to total number of buildings	−689	6,884	2,797	−3,723	−2,402	724	619	−7,862
(33) Total number of buildings	−971	−29,753	−633	9,833	−12,540	7,380	11,558	17,662
(34) Consolidation indicator	5,384	13,100	12,149	−2,967	2,567	−7,592	−4,925	−3,298
(35) Occupancy rate	−110	−18,000	−4,637	1,362	−86	694	4,269	1,416
(36) Number of CBOCs per 1,000 unique patients	4,208	12,558	4,118	2,296	458	−4,133	−5,316	−5,932
(37) Direct patient care FTEs per 1,000 unique patients	4,302	−11,689	7,994	−5,743	5,667	682	−2,886	−4,064
(38) Non-patient care FTEs per 1,000 unique patients	529	−1,842	878	−520	842	206	558	−1,251
(39) LTC beds per 1,000 unique patients	317	2,321	−2,237	−3,099	−2,110	−493	1,088	4,013
(40) Special program beds per 1,000 unique patients	−1,666	1,852	−1,705	3,615	1,511	−4,565	−1,176	−844
Sum of differences—rows (4) through (40)	53,849	−30,221	47,429	−229,267	64,596	−19,288	−18,213	−239,834

Table C.12—continued

	VISN 9	VISN 10	VISN 11	VISN 12	VISN 15	VISN 16	VISN 17	VISN 18
(1) Simulated allocations from AVM with VA DCGs	966,519	753,775	840,181	1,020,783	736,654	1,645,028	907,288	830,773
(2) Unadjusted average allocation	967,279	686,732	867,636	876,677	770,012	1,709,170	904,688	948,652
(3) Difference (1)–(2)	–759	67,043	–27,455	144,107	–33,358	–64,142	2,600	–117,879
Patient characteristics								
(4) Age	1,228	269	–432	–3,550	847	9,232	3,614	–2,171
(5) Income	–123	4,526	–3,285	–2,894	1,544	10,973	3,451	–2,977
(6) Race	5,175	3,588	4,367	3,458	3,665	7,454	–5,650	–10,122
(7) Gender	–553	604	564	185	1,334	1,002	–1,240	–3,088
(8) Martial status	–1,661	1,526	976	1,552	–1,099	–1,772	–1,145	–1,192
(9) Physicians per capita	–3,020	–1,922	609	–3,872	730	–1,482	540	–681
(10) Hospital beds per capita	1,161	–700	–315	1,525	1,376	3,282	–480	–3,027
(11) Rural or urban status	–3,996	1,071	–264	310	–4,811	–3,203	607	–118
(12) Distance to closest facility	262	–5,747	722	–3,187	1,691	6,892	5,162	4,966
(13) Distance to closest CBOC	1,645	–4,606	1,637	–4,290	482	20,879	–1,444	7,714
(14) Priority status	4,794	–2,560	–4,820	491	–4,019	7,261	5,738	4,034
(15) Medicare reliance	9,967	–3,546	–2,886	7,793	6,283	4,248	469	10,565
(16) Medicaid generosity (general)	–3,687	6,611	1,229	3,848	1,676	–19,360	–13,173	–14,539
(17) Medicaid generosity for LTC	–115	–5,022	–1,084	–1,768	–524	6,011	3,123	4,820
(18) VA DCGs health status measure	28,239	50,039	–27,934	94,704	32,538	–48,215	2,020	–31,456
Facility characteristics								
(19) Rural or urban status	2,628	704	–9,049	–2,262	–3,838	–507	2,489	6,689
(20) Residents per full-time MD	–3,454	1,014	2,106	–2,752	–5,521	2,160	–469	801
(21) VA labor index	–15,204	1,195	1,374	15,565	–12,118	–17,725	–19,618	–24,002
(22) Average food cost per bed day	3,204	–1,955	2,019	446	2,712	–1,893	–3,282	–4,283
(23) Energy price ($/million Btus)	–2,575	–604	–3,230	–1,268	–244	–12,678	–8,444	2,509
(24) Contract labor cost share	–456	392	40	–374	286	298	–441	326
(25) Square feet of building space per acre of land	–4,677	–1,666	4,851	6,444	–5,586	25,902	–5,154	–5,947
(26) Square feet of building space per unique patient	3,655	6,348	13,255	32,218	–1,626	–24,502	2,711	–37,610

Table C.12—continued

	VISN 9	VISN 10	VISN 11	VISN 12	VISN 15	VISN 16	VISN 17	VISN 18
(27) Research costs per 1,000 unique patients	-2,416	-1,009	-468	345	-4,899	-3,863	1,232	-2,767
(28) Percentage of funded research	-13,998	4,983	-10,785	5,086	-19,720	-22,905	4,084	-16,758
(29) Average building age	-2,038	-3,362	-4,757	-9,871	-409	-2,901	2,084	1,928
(30) Average building condition	-1,712	132	1,354	568	-440	3,056	1,714	-3,551
(31) Leased square feet per patient	-7,034	13,707	-1,931	-3,043	-10,126	-4,238	4,762	-2,111
(32) Ratio of historic to total number of buildings	2,539	1,811	5,139	-119	-174	-1,531	3,188	1,489
(33) Total number of buildings	5,468	529	2,021	1,450	-7,879	12,220	-4,805	7,092
(34) Consolidation indicator	-7,729	-5,289	-3,258	-1,147	-3,224	-13,432	19,567	-7,566
(35) Occupancy rate	342	3,628	3,411	1,566	6,122	-495	1,582	5,420
(36) Number of CBOCs per 1,000 unique patients	-2,353	-247	-1,560	465	-2,551	-8,174	911	1,415
(37) Direct patient care FTEs per 1,000 unique patients	3,653	4,307	-223	12,627	-8,425	-3,059	2,536	-5,376
(38) Non-patient care FTEs per 1,000 unique patients	572	647	291	1,141	-792	-80	1,056	-956
(39) LTC beds per 1,000 unique patients	1,422	-2,540	244	-3,727	1,795	3,703	-3,606	2,516
(40) Special program beds per 1,000 unique patients	88	187	2,613	-3,555	1,587	3,299	-1,089	138
Sum of differences—rows (4) through (40)	-759	67,043	-27,455	144,106	-33,357	-64,142	2,600	-117,878

Table C.12—continued

	VISN 19	VISN 20	VISN 21	VISN 22	VISN 23
(1) Simulated allocations from AVM with VA DCGs	591,354	944,627	1,075,937	1,167,800	1,027,214
(2) Unadjusted average allocation	550,889	829,897	932,075	1,062,980	1,030,298
(3) Difference (1)–(2)	40,465	114,730	143,862	104,820	–3,084
Patient characteristics					
(4) Age	1,202	4,110	2,379	3,205	–4,953
(5) Income	1,064	3,802	–1,751	–4,293	–9,364
(6) Race	–594	381	–14,669	–6,371	3,870
(7) Gender	–88	–976	–1,695	–679	779
(8) Martial status	–400	1,197	2,788	6,834	–2,892
(9) Physicians per capita	1,280	1,088	1,073	7,198	–155
(10) Hospital beds per capita	–1,719	–3,572	–5,057	–4,812	3,370
(11) Rural or urban status	–3,107	–1,263	2,457	5,664	–7,182
(12) Distance to closest facility	8,285	–820	5,685	–2,148	17,139
(13) Distance to closest CBOC	583	3,026	–583	–8,583	8,826
(14) Priority status	–424	9,144	2,248	–817	–4,835
(15) Medicare reliance	6,707	12,201	5,843	–11,871	11,967
(16) Medicaid generosity (general)	–3,303	–11,700	–10,746	–13,163	18,532
(17) Medicaid generosity for LTC	–1,024	–389	2,035	3,032	–3,877
(18) VA DCGs health status measure	43,058	77,772	399	–8,683	23,606
Facility characteristics					
(19) Rural or urban status	228	–4,632	2,395	2,755	–1,388
(20) Residents per full-time MD	363	4,229	1,510	–5,897	–9,009
(21) VA labor index	–2,882	3,555	66,232	25,205	–5,516
(22) Average food cost per bed day	566	1,825	6,106	9,165	–3,857
(23) Energy price ($/million Btus)	–2,224	–3,464	3,691	3,212	–3,464
(24) Contract labor cost share	521	106	817	731	–340
(25) Square feet of building space per acre of land	–1,135	–6,865	582	–1,015	–8,546
(26) Square feet of building space per unique patient	–4,213	2,688	–9,389	2,080	22,640

Table C.12—continued

	VISN 19	VISN 20	VISN 21	VISN 22	VISN 23
(27) Research costs per 1,000 unique patients	−788	4,194	14,029	12,834	−2,970
(28) Percentage of funded research	−7,199	18,942	51,717	71,669	−5,992
(29) Average building age	−5,120	−5,087	12,097	20,069	−5,638
(30) Average building condition	723	2,304	829	−4,424	−2,607
(31) Leased square feet per patient	4,894	4,152	6,399	8,702	−11,788
(32) Ratio of historic to total number of buildings	725	98	−4,746	−4,552	−214
(33) Total number of buildings	2,265	−2,606	1,277	−5,859	−13,710
(34) Consolidation indicator	−1,394	1,214	−659	1,558	6,943
(35) Occupancy rate	−1,644	1,853	973	2,802	−10,467
(36) Number of CBOCs per 1,000 unique patients	3,938	−2,832	−501	−1,604	4,837
(37) Direct patient care FTEs per 1,000 unique patients	−1,823	3,737	1,626	6,203	−10,046
(38) Non-patient care FTEs per 1,000 unique patients	−426	545	−225	293	−1,465
(39) LTC beds per 1,000 unique patients	1,874	−2,803	−380	235	1,465
(40) Special program beds per 1,000 unique patients	1,694	−425	−923	−3,855	3,218
Sum of differences—rows (4) through (40)	40,465	114,730	143,860	104,819	−3,084

NOTE: Figures shown are in thousands of dollars.

Bibliography

Ash, A. S., R. P. Ellis, G. C. Pope, J. Z. Ayanian, D. W. Bates, H. Burstin, L. I. Iezzoni, E. MacKay, and W. Yu, "Using Diagnosis to Describe Populations and Predict Costs," *Health Care Financing Review,* Vol. 21, No. 3, Spring 2000, pp. 7–28.

Cohen, M. A. and H. L. Lee, "The Determinants of Spatial Distribution of Hospital Utilization in a Region," *Medical Care,* Vol. 23, No. 1, January 1985, pp. 27–38.

Goldman, D. P., A. Leibowitz, J. L. Buchanan, and J. Keesey, "Redistributional Consequences of Community Rating," *Health Services Research,* Vol. 32, 1997, pp. 71–86.

Health Resources and Services Administration, *Area Resource File,* Washington, D.C.: National Center for Health Workforce Analysis, Bureau of Health Professions, 2001.

Manning, W. G., and J. Mullahy, "Estimating Log Models: To Transform or Not to Transform?" *J Health Econ,* Vol. 20, No. 4, July 2001, pp. 461–494.

Pope, G. S., R. P. Ellis, A. S. Ash, J. Z. Ayanian, D. W. Bates, H. Burstin, L. I. Iezzoni, E. Marcantonio, and B. Wu, "Diagnostic Cost Group Hierarchical Condition Category Models for Medicare Risk Adjustment: Final Report," contract, December 21, 2000.

Shannon, G. W., R. L. Bashshur, and J. E. Lovett, "Distance and the Use of Mental Health Services," *Milbank Quarterly,* Vol. 64, No. 2, 1986, pp. 302–330.

Shannon, G. W., J. L. Skinner, and R. L. Bashshur, "Time and Distance: The Journey for Medical Care," *Int J Health Serv,* Vol. 3, No. 2, Spring 1973, pp. 237–244.

U.S. Census Bureau, *Current Population Survey,* Washington, D.C.: U.S. Department of Commerce, 2001.

U.S. Department of Energy, *State Energy Price Report,* Washington, D.C., 2000.

Veterans Equitable Resource Allocation System (VERA Book), 7th Edition, Washington, D.C.: Department of Veterans Affairs, Veterans Health Administration, March 2003, p. 4.

VHA, *Executive Decision Memo, Risk-Adjusted Capitation,* Washington, D.C.: Department of Veterans Affairs, Veterans Health Administration, October 2001.

Wagner, T. H., S. Chen, and P. G. Barnett, "Using Average Cost Methods to Estimate Encounter-Level Costs for Medical-Surgical Stays in the VA," *Medical Care Research and Review,* Vol. 60, No. 3, Supplement, September 2003, pp. 15s–36s.

Wasserman, J., J. Ringel, K. Ricci, J. Malkin, M. Schoenbaum, B. Wynn, J. Zwanziger, S. Newberry, M. Suttorp, and A. Rastegar, *An Analysis of Potential Adjustments to the Veterans Equitable Resource Allocation (VERA) System,* Santa Monica, Calif.: RAND Corporation, MR-1629-DVA, 2003.

Wasserman, J., J. Ringel, B. Wynn, J. Zwanziger, K. Ricci, S. Newberry, B. Genovese, and M. Schoenbaum, *An Analysis of the Veterans Equitable Resource Allocation (VERA) System,* Santa Monica, Calif.: RAND Corporation, MR-1419-DVA, 2001.

Weiss, J. E., M. R. Greenlick, and J. F. Jones, "Determinants of Medical Care Utilization: The Impact of Spatial Factors," *Medical Care,* Vol. 8, No. 6, November–December 1970, pp. 456–462.

Welch, W. P., "Improving Medicare Payments to HMOs: Urban Core Versus Suburban Ring," *Inquiry,* Vol. 26, 1989, pp. 62–71.

Yu, W., and P. G. Barnett, *Research Guide to Decision Support System National Cost Extracts: 1998–2000,* Menlo Park, Calif.: VA Health Economics Resource Center, 2000.